COMMUNALISM AND COMMUNAL RIOTS IN INDIA

COMMUNALISM AND COMMUNAL RIOTS IN INDIA

A HISTORICAL PERSPECTIVE

Dr. Pravin Kumar

Shyam Lal College
University of Delhi
Delhi

ABHIJEET PUBLICATIONS
DELHI 110094

ABHIJEET PUBLICATIONS
2/46 Tukhmeerpur Extension
Delhi 110094
Phones: 011-22960492, 65698474
e-mail: abhijeetpublication@gmail.com
abhijeet_singh1@indiatimes.com

COMMUNALISM AND COMMUNAL RIOTS IN INDIA

First Published 2009

ISBN 978-93-80031-00-2

PRINTED IN INDIA

Published by J.K. Singh fo Abhijeet Publications, Delhi 110094, Lasertypeset by Gaurav Graphics, Delhi and Printed as Himanshu Printers, Delhi.

PREFACE

Historians have attempted to understand the complex question of Indian partition in 1947, the evolving structure of communalism and subsequent riots in their own ways. Scholars like Gyanendra Pandey in his book *Remembering Partition* has tried to blend history with memory to unearth even the forgotten aspect of Indian partition to ensure a comprehensive understanding of the events of 1947. Not only the enormity of the event has been taken into consideration, but also he has tried to decode and deconstruct the process of re-making of the community as the result of the experiences of violence, a particular community or communities had to go through during such tragic eventualities. In such instances, "violence too becomes a language that constitutes—and reconstitutes—the subject". Mushirul Hasan, in his own way, has also proposed to study the "mind" of the people of both the communities with a long history of plural heritage during the years, prior to the partition. Why did a society with a tradition of strong pluralism become the site of unprecedented cataclysmic events during these years—remained the issue that Prof. Hasan tries to sort out in his edited book *Inventing Boundaries*. Sucheta Mahajan tries to tackle the issue of communalism and partition in the context of crystallizing Indian nationalist pressure and the adjusting and re-adjusting imperialist position of English overlords. In yet another refreshing enquiry on the subject, Joya Chatterjee, in the book *Bengal Divided,* re-evaluates the events of 1946-47 and in the process she successfully underlines those social and political processes that led to the demand for partition in a Muslim majority province of Bengal.

Some of the works underlined above suggest a departure as far as questions on nature of researches on communalism and communal riots are concerned. Historians have now started favouring to work on interpreting the short-term fluctuations in the history of communalism. However, this does not mean that the works centred to make a clear-cut understanding of the long-term trends that culminated into sprouting of communal consciousness, its crystallization and gradual consolidation are irrelevant. Surely, *Communalism in Modern India* of Bipan Chandra and *The Construction of Communalism in Colonial North India* by Gyanendra Pandey are worthy and valuable works for the students of history in their own ways. Communalism and Communal riots in Delhi in 1947, a topic undertaken by me belongs to the category of works that tries to concentrate on the short-term variables that made Delhi a site of violence and riots during the year 1947. Surely, Delhi in 1947 meant many things. It was not only an important urban center of colonial India, but also a political nerve center, the temperature and pulse rate of which determined both, the fever of Indian nationalism and waning beat of

British imperialism. It symbolized also the cultural amalgamation of the so-called 'Hindu India', 'Muslim India' as well as 'modernized' British India. The composite culture of India was in a way, represented by 'Old Delhi', the 'Imperial Delhi' and the 'Nationalist Delhi'. All the political forces along with 'Hindu Right Wing' and all time rebellious Sikhs had their stakes here. The Muslim League under Jinnah wanted to legitimize its claim of Pakistan. The changing mindset in 1947 in this direction meant more riots and the greater sense of subsequent insecurity in the Muslim mind and thus the message that Muslims as a community was not very secure in 'Hindu India'. The Hindu Right Wing, aiming for 'purified' Hindu Mother Land, was up to remodel Delhi in accordance with their own vision. British officials, a perfect broker as they were, wanted to maintain *status quo* to underline their claim of good administration and to create an indirect impression that India was no more than a 'geographical expression' without British overlordship. Evidently they might be trying for the British brand of 'Balkanized India' as was clear from their game-plan.

It was this background that made Delhi a center of communal violence in 1947. As we all know, the ultimate expression of communal hatred has been the 'riots'. For an average individual, communalism and communal riots are synonymous. The scholars of history, however, distinguish those categories from each other. Communalism, for them, has been a long-term evolutionary process which at first assumes an ideological makind and the ideological setting gradually evolves and creates its social base to make the consciousness popular and strongly footed. The social 'class' starts radiating their specific ideological positions in their organized political behaviour. A structured and defined political behaviour then demands the creation of a specific political (communal) organization. The political-communal organization, thus emerged, starts radiating 'signs' and 'symbols' of a particular kind of consciousness, resulting finally into different communal groups/parties, a result of engineered 'social cleavages'. This process finally finds its ultimate expression in riots, bloodshed and further strengthening of social divide on communal lines. From Bipan Chandra to Gyanendra Pandey, from Sociologists to Economic Reductionists, from Imperialists to Marxists, all of them try to explain communalism and communal riots in more or less in similar theoretical constructs.

But this is not a proper place to go deep into these theoretical constructs and their differential use by different scholars. What is simply intended to underline the fact that a macro-trends, as underlined above, might have contributed to growing communalization of Delhi politics in 1947 and also to the subsequent riots. More than the macro trends, I am more inclined to concentrate on 'other variables' that explains the fluctuations in the political/communal climate of Delhi in 1947. As far as the macro trends are concerned they are well known and do not warrant specific attention.

As far as the pattern of communal riots in Delhi - 1947 is concerned, two waves of the 'riots' can easily be observed. The first wave lasted slightly longer, i.e., from March to May, covering a span of three months. The second wave, generally termed as September riots, obviously precipitated in the month of September. Apart from these two waves the sporadic occurrence of the riots of relatively lesser magnitude can be witnessed almost throughout the year. In this sense, the year 1947 for Delhi was the year of 'communal riots'. In a charged atmosphere throughout the period under study, the fluctuations in communal consciousness over time is bound to be difficult to measure very accurately. Another important limitation in this case is the determination of the extent of the role played by economics in the making of the riots.

Still, economics played a role in this process. The economic situation in 1946-47 helped in the process of social alienation and thus broadened the base of criminalization, and also of communalization, as boundaries of both processes started blurring during this period. If one compares records, the rising trend is more or less visible. Wheat witnessed the rise of one anna from six annas, maize Rs 2 and 8 annas, barley Rs one, etc. And these are official statistics. In the real markets, rise was bound to be sharper than it looks to us. What is important here to note is a sharper rise of prices in cheap commodities than those of the costlier ones. The prices of maize and barley rose sharply than the other commodities. In other words, the cost of living of the poor people became dearer which helped in the process of social alienation. This is not to deny that the wages of the labourers and artisans also went up, but not to the extent it was warranted. Also larger sections of the lower classes consisted of half employed or even unemployed people. Their economic position worsened gradually. In the event of riots, these people became the readymade cadre of communal violence as riots provided them means to 'earn' and loot.

So far as the privileged classes are concerned. They did not suffer from hunger and malnutrition. The police report finds the business community in flourishing conditions owing to speculative activities, hoarding and profiteering. Thus emerged a powerful class of black marketers and contractor, ready to cash on every event and episode politically. Thus there emerged a bi-polar structure—one as socially and economically powerful elites and another as over-exploited and volatile steps, both of them ready to exploit 'riots' to their own end. In other words, economics had a certain role in rise of communalism and communal riots in Delhi.

More than economics, there were other factors which played a more decisive role in rise of communal temperature and making of the riots. One such important variable was misuse of religious sites. Unnecessary controversies around them was created and contesting public opinion, manufactured to arise the sentiment of the masses. Since religion and religious sites in those days, were synonymous, the abuse of religious sites therefore meant the abuse of religion itself. In this background, the abusing of such sites becomes a political and strategic weapon in the hands of the brokers of religion which they used to stimulate religious sentiments and to make innocent mind strained in communal colour. Thus communalism should not be understood only as a 'false or negative cosciousness', as many modern historians believe, but also as 'an engineered, stimulated and imposed consciousness' under the cover of which rests the innocent mind. The moment we succeed in melting this engineered, stimulated and imposed mask of communalization, the process of rationalization and thus secularization is bound to begin. In other words, even the sharply divided societies on communal lines had in-built capacity to reverse the process, if the political leadership is willing to do that. In other it might well be a counter-productive step if one is willing to invent the structural constructs of communalism.

The process to communalize the human mind through this process might be witnessed in 1947-Delhi. In Tughlak Road incident of December 1946, unnecessary controversy was created over building of a roof in a mosque of Mochi Bagh (Moti Bagh). A similar controversy was raised by Muslims of Kishanganj where a *chabutara* with an appearance of mosque was created and walled off. Again, Hindus of Ram Lila Ground area demolished a mosque and built a temple there. Similar situation was created at Mosque of Takya near Turkman Gate, Mosque Haju Aki Jan, near Ghanta-Ghar, Rajpur Road Mosque, Takia Bela Road Mosque near Civil Lines, etc. The modality to communalize mind was very simple. First, a site was chosen, it was then given a religious identify. A counter-claim on such sites was then bound to be created by another community. The process usually culminated into a kind of *Namaj-Sankha* controversy. In other words, interested parties started playing the politics of religion on the question of such controversial sites giving birth to the process, culminating into communal construction. The real motive behind all such exercise was not only political, but a serious land-grabbing activity was also involved in the process.

Press, posters and other popular tracts often play a crucial role in the process. The high-pitched campaigns carried out through this medium generally helped in raising the communal fever at even more intense level. Communalism, on its part, feeded itself on popular media. Colonial administration remained at best manipulative which is clear from the time-gap between beginning of the politics of propaganda and the official reaction against it. *Cartoon Controversy of Delhi,* in *Dawn,* a Muslim paper printed in Delhi, could provide an example. The first cartoon seemed to suggest that the North-West India (a Muslim majority zone) was asleep while the Hindu lion, seated with the corpses of Bihar Muslims, was enjoying the moment. The second cartoon suggested that the people of North-West India still remained unmoved to this act except sending two medical missions. Though these two cartoons were treated as 'the most provocative' and the Chief Commissioner of Delhi was requested by the Punjab Government to "warn the editoer the *Dawn*" against printing of such cartoons. But Delhi administration hardly initiated any substantial action except a demand of a security worth Rs. 3,000/- from the keeper/publisher of *Dawn.* Though administration itself suggested three precautionary measures, but they were yet to act accordingly. Similarly, events in Punjab were disturbing, and they featured prominently in all sections of the Press "without restraint", desirable and/or promised. A move was made to include some of the newspapers to the "censorship list" which included *The Hindustan Times, The Dawn, The National Call The Janata Weekly, The Daily Tej, Riyasat, Ansari, Anjan, Payam, Watch* and *Swarajya.* But nothing materialized up to first three quarters of the year 1947. Only in October 1947, the pre-censorship orders under Section 4(b) of the Press (Special Powers No. 2) Ordinance 1947 were served on the editors, printers and publishers of *Dawn, Hindu Outlook, Jung, Wahadat, Alamah, Naya Daur, Aj* and *Balajit. Aj* was warned for publishing objectionable material regarding communal riots. However, the timing of the action is important. Administration did not take any initiative until two waves of communal riots had already passed. After September riots, by the time all the damages were already done, the administration suddenly started becoming active. Reason behind this activity was obviously the 'transfer of power' from British Crown to the hands of Indians themselves.

Communal riots are not the mechanical result of growing communal consciousness. It, in fact, needs carriers/mediums to incite and stimulate otherwise fluid state of popular mind. Communal organizations, thus acquire significance in this process. The process was true even in the case of 1947-Delhi. The important communal organizations, active in Delhi in 1947, were the Hindu National Guards, The Muslim National Guards, The Akali Dal, the Akal Regiment, the Sikh National Volunteer Corps, etc. In the ever-changing political scenario, all of them tried to pose themselves as the real protectors of the interests of the respective communities. In the name of protecting their respective community interests, each of them started projecting the community it represented, above the composite social structure, and thus started creating 'cracks' in the social fabric. In this process, Indian identity of the people of Delhi was lost to their separate and individualistic identities of Hindus, Muslims, Sikhs, etc. This transformation remained one of the important reasons of the growth of communalism and incidence of communal riots in Delhi in 1947.

After the Paharganj riot in November 1946; it was decided by conservative Hindus to create Hindu National Guards to protect the 'special Hindu interests'. The Muslim National Guards were already in existence with the membership approaching near 700. Many Muslim leaders had already started complaining that 'insufficient interest is being taken in them' by the Muslim population. There was an urgent need to reverse the process. Apart from the Muslim National Guards, Khaksars were also active in Delhi. By that time, R.S.S. had the strength of about 3000 of whom all but 500 were in urban area of Delhi and cantonment. Though all branches of the Sangh had organizing physical exercises in their sakhas regularly, but they were eager to transform this defensive mechanism into active one, so that their existence might be legitimized among the Hindus, an essential step if R.S.S. at all, wanted to expand its social base.

In the meantime, the local Muslim League was facing an acute crisis. No confidence motion against the President and the Secretary of Delhi Provincial Muslim League had already been moved. The leaders were apprehensive that internal fighting and inactivity would soon render it virtually moribund. A 'radical' programme became the cry of the time for the League. The 'events or Punjab' and R.S.S. proposal to hold a big conference in Delhi provided that opportunity. The Punjab Government's decision to ban R.S.S. and the Muslim National Guards caused a good deal of excitement. The subsequent withdrawal of ban from R.S.S., a surprise step of the Government of Punjab created a sense of concern among the Muslims.

These developments also galvanized Hindu communal .organizations. Banning of RSS in Punjab was one of the reasons. The hammering by the Punjab Government convinced the Hindu Right Wing in Delhi about the need of strengthening their organisational strength. Banning of their proposed rally in Delhi by the Government angered them. Delhi's butcher strike supported by the Muslim League and their well attended meetings as well as a jointly planned processions with the Jamiat-ul-Quresh, all, helped the All India Hindu Mahasabha to conclude that the League was planning/preparing for 'direct action', resulting in a resolution warning the country for that eventuality. Hindus and Sikhs of Delhi, therefore, observed on 11th March 1947 an anti-Pakistan Day. An Anti-Pakistan Council came into existence with children, young students and conservative Hindus as the members. Madho Rao Golvalkar, the Sangh Chief in his speeches and private meetings gave strict instructions that all 'outsiders' should leave Delhi without delay. Refugees from Punjab brought harrowing tales of atrocities and its accounts in the press, particularly those from special correspondents of various papers, sharpened the tension. The determination of the Muslim League to celebrate Pakistan Day on 23rd March, 1947 made the environment more explosive. Even the members of Akali Dal started becoming active in the name of defending the Sikh community in Delhi. In the mean time, All India Dharam Sangh under the leadership of Swami Karpatriji Maharaj declared his 'Dharamyudha campaign' and his memorandum to the members of Central Government, which contained 5 specific demands namely, (a) cow protection, (b) Akhand Bharat, (c) independence of religion, (d) sanctity to temples, and (e) representation to Sanatani Hindus in constitution-making body and all its committees.

Role of Police was naturally very crucial in this context. It was one of the pillars over which the superstructure of the mighty British Empire in India rested. It restored law and order, suppressed the rebellious voice of over-exploited Indian masses, provided a defensive shield in the mechanism of colonial drain and created a myth of all powerful British apparatus/state in the minds of common Indian folks. It was successful in playing such a crucial role because it acted as a living organ of British imperialism. But the gradual Indianization of colonial police meant gradual 'injection of mind' in it. Individuals in police started thinking, became conscious of their (community) interests, their emotions and their political surroundings. It became visible in the last days of imperialism. For Delhi, it meant that in a communally charged atmosphere of Delhi, police started behaving 'differently'.

That police started playing partisan role in Delhi is evident from the Paharganj riot only. The point is clear from the statistics of police after-action where no Muslim was arrested; only Hindus and Sikhs were penalized. But pro-Muslim bias of the police remained visible until April 1947 only. After that, pressure from Home Ministry forced police to become sympathetic to Hindu and Sikh causes. The Home Ministry under Sardar Ballava Bhai Patel started recognizing itself as representing the interests primarily of Hindus. This fact was evident from the questionnaire prepared by the Home Ministry regarding the modality of representation of different communities in Delhi Police. Its subsequent suggestion to balance the Hindu and Sikh representations in the Police with that of the Muslims was a significant official move. The Hon'ble Minister, "though recognizes that the wholesale changes cannot be brought about simultaneously ... he thought, however, a period of six or eight months should be sufficient...." In other words a 'nexus between Congress at the Centre, the Delhi police and the Hindu communalists' cannot be ruled out. Though, details of this nexus could be clearly understood, if one goes through the chapter on police in the book.

What all these details suggest, is the transformation of Delhi into a site of communal disturbances in 1947. Though macro-trends had a role to play in this transformation, but more than 'macro-trends', it was micro-tendencies, namely, the process that made religious sites controversial, the kind of role — police, press and communal organizations played and the way Delhi administration chose to act or unact during the sensitive period of the year 1947, that clearly explains the rise of communalism and unfortunate incidents of communal riot in the year of our study. It was the process underlined above that made Delhi a sensitive place to live in 1947.

Prof. G.P. Sharma, Head, Dept. of History, Jamia Millia Islamia, contributed a lot as my guide to the making of this work. His advice and words of encouragement did wonder to my work ethics and sparked many ideas that helped me in handling this complex subject. I am grateful for his sincere support and deep interest in this work.

I express my gratitude and thankfulness to Shri Anil Dutta Mishra who has facilitated the publishing of this work and offered many helps and suggestions for this work.

Besides this my sincere gratitudeness is on record for my family members, fellow academicians on the subject and the authorities of Shyamlal College and Delhi University.

Dr. Pravin Kumar

CONTENTS

Preface *v*

1. Introduction 1
2. Controversial Religious Sites 18
3. Press 32
4. Communal Organizations 48
5. Police 68
6. Conclusion: Communalism and Communal Riots 93

Appendix I 119

Appendix II 126

Appendix III 131

Appendix IV 138

Appendix V 140

Select Bibliography 149

1

INTRODUCTION

Delhi in 1947 meant many things. It was not only an important urban centre of colonial India but also a political nerve centre, the temperature and pulse rate of which determined the 'fever of Indian nationalism' and 'waning beat' of British imperialism. It symbolized also the cultural amalgamation of the so-called 'Hindu India', 'Muslim India' as well as the 'modernized' British India. The composite culture of India was in a way represented by 'Old Delhi', the 'Imperial Delhi', and the 'Nationalist Delhi'. All the political forces along with 'Hindu Right Wing' and all time rebellious Sikhs had their stakes here. The Muslim League wanted to legitimize its claim of Pakistan which meant more riots and greater sense of insecurity for the Muslims and thus the message that Muslim as a community was not very secure in 'Hindu India'. The Hindu right wing, aiming for 'purified' Hindu mother land, was trying to have Delhi as the model of their goal. British, as a perfect broker, wanted to maintain status quo to establish their claim of good administration emphasizing that India was no more than a 'geographical expression' without British overlordship. Evidently, they might be trying for the British brand of 'Balkanized India', as was clear from their game-plan.

To understand the modality of the interaction of above-mentioned forces in 1947, it seems necessary to go deep into the immediate background. Under this logic, the understanding of the political, administrative, economic and communal climate of Delhi in 1946 became important for the proper understanding of the communal situation in Delhi in 1947. Our main concern here would, however, be of communal atmosphere, law and order situation, police administration and other related matters.

Law and Order Situation

Going through the official documents[1] one may notice the improvement of law and order situation in Delhi in 1946 if one compares it to that of 1945. In a report of DCO to CCO all kinds of crimes dealt with by the police in 1946 was 16,434 (true cases) compared with 13755 in 1945, a decrease of 2679 cases.[2] For the same period figures for the 'reported' crime were 16321 against 18701, a decrease of 2380.[3] The 'official' explanation for the decrease in reported and true cases appear to be due to three main reasons:[4]

(a) Lesser registration of cycle thefts;

(b) The practice of investigating many cases of similar type in one First Information Report; and

(c) The imposition of curfew for a good portion of the year.

What is important here is that even the 'official'[5] interpretation of the condition of Delhi was not that of an 'improved condition'. Despite the unimaginative explanation of (a) and (b), the third explanation is very revealing. Even after the imposition of curfew for a good portion of the year', the number of actual crimes (16434) was very substantial which proves the deteriorating condition of law and order in Delhi province. From the police point of view, the figure might be satisfactory but a rational mind can easily conclude the 'worsening' condition of Delhi and 'charged' public opinion from the very explanation. The report points to the subversive activities of the labour classes[6] as well as the 'communal lawlessness'[7]. However one can again notice an upward trend. The actual figure of the magnitude of their charged mind is difficult to quantify.

The following table gives an idea of the crime position in Delhi between 1937 and 1946. There is a decline in the crime rate midway though the period reaching the lowest mark of 7625 cases in 1942. The most plausible reason seems to be the Quit India movement, which broke out in the same year thus diverting the attention of the rioters. An upward tendency in crime would be noticeable from 1943. The official explanation of the growing trend were[8]

Year	*Reported*	*True cases*
1937	14,795	13,960
1938	15,612	13,080
1939	13,521	13,632
1940	12,225	12,553
1941	13,601	12,827
1942	8,000	7,625
1943	16,349	15,013
1944	18,552	15,119
1945	18,701	19,113
1946	16,321	16,434

Source: The Police Report.[9]

(i) Increase in population especially in the urban area.

(ii) Acute communal tension resulting in communal riots.

(iii) The frequent imposition of curfew and other restrictive orders.

(iv) Wide spread of labour unrest resulting in strikes and 'other unlawful activities' (potentially dangerous group, may transform into rioting mobs).

(v) Increase in crime due to violation of price control and rationing orders.

The law and order condition in Delhi was getting increasingly worse becomes clear from other statistics of offences. While going through the crime chart one may note that 'increases' were recorded in almost all kinds of offences excepting physical assaults and counterfeiting. The data given below shows emphatically that there was a growing incidence of violence and this increasing trend lead us to conclude the 'continuous swelling of the volatile population'. This type of social structuring is also important when one is dealing with communal problem in a given point of time. It is because this section of the population of society provides the base and cadre for communal organizations the ground for rioting.

Offences	*1945*	*1946*	*Fluctuations*
Thefts	2752	2905	+153
Burglary	789	1037	+ 248
Misappropriation	139	154	+15
Robbery	53	66	+13
Mischief	8	13	+5

Other hurts	64	60	-4
Cheating	94	118	+24
Grievous hurt	64	95	+31
Kidnapping & abduction	30	31	+1
Attempt to murder	15	42	+27
Murder	28	43	+15
Counterfeiting coins	5	1	-4
Rioting	14	42	-28
Dacoity	7	9	+2

Source: Police Report, 1947, DCO, file.

The economic situation of 1946 helped the process of social alienation and thus broadened the base of criminalisation, and also of communalization, both of which were closely related as has already been hinted above. The prices of almost all the commodities were increasing steadily as it is clear from the following statistics.[10]

			1945			*1946*	
Commodity	*Per maund*	*Rs*	*As.*	*Ps*	*Rs.*	*As.*	*Ps.*
Wheat	"	10	1	0	10	2	0
Gram	"	8	2	0	8	8	0
Maize	"	6	6	0	8	14	0
Barley	"	6	2	0	7	2	0
Bajra	"	7	8	0	7	8	0

The important conclusion, which the official explanation has ignored, is relatively faster rise in the prices of cheaper commodities than those of the costlier commodities. The prices of maize and barley, the cheapest of the cereals, grew most sharply than those of wheat and gram. That is to say that[11] the cost of living of poor people became dearer and thus helped the process of social alienation. Although 'the wages of labour and artisan classes went up', the real value of wages was offset by the rising price of essential commodities. This is indicated by the rise in crime graph and communalization of the politics shows that it was not so.

So far as the privileged classes ere concerned, they did not suffer from hunger and malnutrition. The report[12] finds the *business community in flourishing* condition, owing to speculative activities like creating artificial rise in the prices, hoarding and profiteering. This created a powerful class of 'black marketeers and contractors'. Contractors grew richer because of government contracts connected with the war. Thus emerged a powerful 'political class' resulting from 'blackmarketeer-contractor nexus' ready to cash on any event and episode politically. Thus, there emerged a 'bi-polar' structure of two opposite classes, i.e., the socially alienated, over worked, over-strained working class and marketeers and contractors, conscious of their economic power and always ready to exploit every opportunity to make political and economic gains, on the other. This postulate may be supported by the statistics of crime. While the instances of true cases registered in city police stations increased substantially (+ 99 + 470 = + 569) in one year between 1945 and 1946, the true cases registered in the rural police station rose by just + 2.[13] Hauz Qazi, Sabzimandi, Qarol Bagh, Civil Lines, Tughlaqa Road and Cantonments were the most disturbed areas while in Narela, Nangloi, Najafgarh, Mehrauli and Shahadara, the situation remained static and under control.[14]

This trend was officially described in the following lines:[15] (i) Greater number of traffic offences; (ii) offences against various controls and rationing orders which are common in urban area but absent in rural area; (iii) the greater concentration of 'bad characters' in the urban areas; (iv) promulgation of certain laws which are in force only in the urban areas; and (v) greater tendency to report cases in urban areas than in rural areas. The above description has its own limitations, for it may explain the greater magnitude of crime in the urban police stations, but it cannot explain the fluctuations in crime rate over time.

[B] 1946 : Through the Mirror of Events

The official documents[16] mention that the increasing intensity of criminalization was due to 'disturbances of the 7th March 1946 and also communal lawlessness throughout the year'. It further points out[17] 'the riots on 7th March were mainly sponsored by the Communist Party as a protest against Victory Celebration'. The point which was however not probed is whether there was any possibility of transforming the 'protest celebration' into the 'communalization of the politics of Delhi', for there must be a very substantial overlapping between 'communist' mass-base and 'communal' mass-base.

The 7th March was being celebrated as 'Victory Day', but the 'radicals' boycotted the celebrations. All the political parties of Delhi geared up themselves for this event and made their respective strategies. The Congress Party decided that it will boycott the Victory Celebrations and will not make any demonstration. Students Congress[19] had to adhere to the Congress Programme. Students Federation[20] geared up themselves to sell black badges and black flags, to persuade the students to participate in the protest and to move about in the city urging citizens to observe hartal. Leftist Groups[21] were ready to hold a public meeting on Queen's Garden at 3 P.M., in which destitutes and volunteers had to tie bricks to their bellies and move about in the city shouting slogans of "Hai Bhook - Hai Bhook" and to visit finally Faiz Bazar at the time of military march past. The Communist Party made an extensive programme:[22] it decided to organize meetings at Roshan Ara Garden and Urdu Park, to organize strikes at Birla, Jama and Delhi Cloth Mills, to take out processions from Roshan Ara Garden via Bara Hindu Rao, Bara Tooti, Lahori Gate, Clock Tower and to reach Jama Masjid; to persuade mill owner; tramway employees and employers of the municipality to observe hartal, and Miss Sarala Gupta, a communist, had to take out a procession of women in black burqas and black sarees. The Muslim League also decided[23] to boycott the Victory Celebration but they decided not to make "any demonstrations".

What is important here is to analyze the 'varied' attitude of the different political parties towards the Victory Day Celebration. While the Communist Party along with Congress Socialist Party and other left oriented people were highly critical of the Victory Day Celebration which was very clear from their slogan "Hai-Bhook, Hai-Bhook" the Muslim League definitely was less antagonistic. This differentially of attitude, indirectly hints at the 'inherent cracks' in the anti-government response. It was very easy for the anti-social elements, the active participants in the protest, as evident from police FIR[24] and official documents,[25] to transform the protest demonstration into communal rioting.

Now, let us concentrate on the happenings of the protest celebration. It is not to suggest that the government was totally unaware of the possible reaction of the Victory Celebration. The Home Department had already required[26] from the Commissioner of Police in the context of the recent disturbances in Bombay, Calcutta, Karachi and Madras, information regarding steps taken to prevent such a situation in Delhi. The Senior Superintendent of Police wrote to the Chief Police Commissioner[27] that there was no evidence that the major political parties [the Congress and the League] had been trying to exploit the recent disturbances in Bombay and elsewhere but the lumpen elements and rowdy students of the town as well as few Congress Socialists under the control of Shankar Lal Bansal and some assorted communists were also ever ready to exploit any situation which would bring embarrassment to the authorities. One might note here that the Muslim League in any form was not mentioned.

On the 7th March 1946, the Victory Day was opposed by the political parties following their own strategies. But at about 2 P.M. as expected, crowds of rioters in Chandni Chowk broke down the victory arches[28] and set fire to them. A police van on patrol was stopped and burnt. The rioting spread throughout Delhi and several buildings, including the Town Hall, ration office, the railway station, terminal tax post etc. were burnt. The police on duty was obstructed by rioters and brick-bats were freely thrown at them.[29]

This was very dangerous from the administrative point of view. Even W. Christie, the Chief Commissioner, agreed that "the disturbances in Delhi during the Victory Day Celebrations ... were definitely organized by excited elements and by the

Communists".[30] Still, "no concerted action against such troublesome elements" wrote the Chief Commissioner,[31] was considered advisable. The result was that the culprits, the antisocial elements, readymade sellers of violence and rioting people were left roaming in their playground, for disturbing the secular fabric of Delhites. One innocent observer might treat it as an accident, but for a regular viewer, familiar with the shrewdness of British administrators and their long-term objective, it is difficult to characterize that merely as an administrative failure. Delhi, in any case, had to pay for this or rather was forced to pay for it.

This failure naturally led to the Lodhi Colony controversy and communal riot in the area under Faiz Bazar police station. Lodhi Colony was entirely populated by government servants, situated at a distance of nearly four miles away from the city and there were no regular means of communication to and from the colony. During the day while all males were in office, the children and ladies of their families were left alone and unprotected. Even a few criminals or rioters could terrorize them and create mischief in their absence. fear arose in the colony because a fairly large number of Muslim students from Aligarh came to stay in vacant quarters in Clerks' Colony[32] which resulted in a very serious "adverse effect on communal relation". Hindu clerks became very excited and "windy", so much so that for several nights they would not go to bed and remained outside their quarters in batches shouting at full pitch of their voice to keep up their courage.[33] This resulted, found Christie,[34] not only in maintaining their own windiness but in putting the wind up to other people. And the process of communalization was rapid for 'these Muslim students were exceedingly provocative and went about shouting provocative slogans in the Lodhi Colony area'.[35] The rumour was also that the Muslims of the colony have collected weapons such as lathis, daggers, knives, etc. in quarters number 39A/20, 598B, 633B and the undesirable people reside in these quarter during the night'.[36] It was also 'understood that a large number of *goondas* have come from outside and are being harboured in village Nizamuddin which is at a distance of only a few furlongs from the colony'.[37] Tension became so apparent that Mahatma Gandhi was forced to re-establish communal harmony.

In the next month, on the 20th May 1946, at about 7 P.M., some Hindu boys including members of the Rashtriya Swayam Sewak Sangh were playing games on the Ram Lila Grounds, near Harihar Temple. All of a sudden, a kid, belonging to a Muslim which was grazing in the vicinity went to the Ground where the games were proceeding. One of the members of the RSS carried the kid off the ground and threw the child resulting into abuse and counter abuse between the owner of the kid and members of the Sangh. A Hindu-Muslim riot developed[38] following the same modality.

What is implicit here is that the police behaved in an irresponsible manner. Nothing serious was done to nab the *goondas* and anti-social elements. The result was that the makers of riots and disturbances were roaming freely in the streets of Delhi, ready to exploit each and every opportunity to their advantage. Many arms were stolen during the year including pistols, revolvers, B.L. gun, DDBL gun, rifles,[39] etc. The list of illicit arms, that had been seized by the police (and they are marginal in respect of the total quantity of the arms) included Tomy spears and daggers,[40] point to the ability of misorients in paralyzing the whole administration and pushing Delhi into abyss.

And this trend finally found its culmination in Paharganj riot in November. It happened when a number of Hindus in the Paharganj area released a cow being taken through Chuna Mandi Bazar to be slaughtered on the occasion of Id.[41] The previous evening a dispute had already taken a shape regarding the route by which cows should be taken for slaughtering.[42] There was no specifically prescribed route for these cows to be taken for slaughtering because this was a comparatively recently built up area.

There existed, however, a custom according to which these cows were taken through Paharganj Bazar and Chuna Mandi to the slaughter house. Mr. Desh Bandhu Gupta and Baba Bachittar Singh were taking a prominent part[43] in the agitation. They wished that cows should be taken further up the Paharganj Road and along the new road known as Chitra Gupta Road. But they were unable to reach an agreement. Meanwhile, the cows were standing on the cross road of Chuna Mandi and on both sides large and angry crowds were collected. Now the Senior Superintendent of Police, Delhi decided to take the cows through the route suggested by Mr. Desh Bandhu Gupta and Baba Bachittar Singh, that further along Paharganj Bazar and then by Chitra Gupta Road.[44]

Meanwhile, there was a great deal of abuse and counter-abuse, shouting and counter-shouting. Angry Hindus and Sikhs finally rushed out and barred the way and started the rioting. The police force under Robinson opened fire and only after about 30 rounds of firing, the police succeeded in carrying the cow to the slaughter house. Dr. Hussain Baksh, a leading physician, in the process, was injured seriously. Indeed at first it was thought by the police that he had been killed on the spot. The problem of routes for carrying the cows to the slaughter house can easily be surmised as one of the reasons for worsening communal harmony in Delhi.[45]

The most important thing, however, is to understand the police response towards the communal disturbances, one must note when going through the description of the communal eruption in Paharganj area.[46] Mr. M.D. Robinson was present throughout the process of the eruption and he did nothing definite to diffuse the crisis. Firing was ordered only when the situation had gone out of hand. Whether this was again an administrative failure or a 'deliberate' administrative inaction is open to question. But the fact remains that "a total of 4 upper subordinates, 12 head constables and 85 constables"[47] was far behind the strength actually needed to control such a situation. But supplementation of the forces was "impossible", argued Robinson, for it meant further "bleeding[48] to already strained reserves". Not to strain more reserve of police force was thought to be a better choice than to stop the rioting. In the light of the above deduction of arguments, it seems improper to treat the police failure only a mere accident and nothing more.

Again, going through the list[49] of community-wise arrests of rioters, we may find another interesting bias. Since the Paharganj riot was the result of community clashes between the Hindus and Sikhs on the one hand and the Muslims on the other, the arrests, the preventive measure to stop the further communalization, should be representative of all the three communities. The realities,[50] however, were that out of 10 arrests all were either Hindus or Sikhs but not a single Muslim was arrested. Was it an accident, once again, or some deliberate 'latent' policy of the local administrators? One hardly needs the answer to such a self-revealing question. One may ask this question in the context of casualties that resulted from the rioting, 9 were either Hindus or Sikhs and 7 were Muslims.[51] This is why the Home Department complained[52] against the manner the whole affair of Paharganj was dealt with by the local administrators. A Home member was of the opinion that "the matter should have been taken to a much higher level ... and at a much earlier date when it was known that opposition was likely to develop to the passage of the cows through the route proposed ... when a decision had been taken, there should have been no further parlaying, and the compliance with the decision should have been firmly enforced ...", again adequate precautions do not seem to have been taken in the area Multani Dhanda where stabbing subsequently occurred.[53]

Arrests	*Hindus*	*Muslims*	*Sikhs*	*Total*
1. Those arrested for Actual participation	6	No one	1	7
2. Those arrested under suspicion	2	No one	-	2
3. Those arrested under Arms Act	1	No one	-	1

These incidents show a trend of continuity throughout the year 1946. All the three incidents, we have dealt with, were expected, and could have been anticipated and a determined administration, with a huge administrative apparatus should have acted as a 'power brake'. If one goes through the correspondence[54] between the Home Department and the Chief Commissioner and the Chief Commissioner and Police authorities in the Paharganj case,[55] it is not impossible to find out the 'fissure' or 'crack' in administrative hierarchy. One point is very certain that the police did not behave in a very responsible manner. Again, that no substantial actions were taken against rowdy and goonda elements, acted as 'carriers' of communalism in all the three incidents. After successfully assessing their role, one is dragged to the conclusion that the police under local administrators were guided by the policies or motives other than administrative. It is important especially in the background of the strong administrative consciousness that administration of Delhi has a heavier responsibility, for Delhi was the seat of government;[56] that anything happened there would have repercussions on the rest of India;[57] that all the magistrates and police officers should have continued to discharge their duty with full consciousness of the importance and gravity of the tasks entrusted to them[58] and, therefore, that 'there is a continued need of firm action... .[59] But that was not done and it played a crucial role in the genesis of communal riots along with such factors as lack of agreement between the major political parties and strained relations between various communities and many others.

REFERENCES

1. *Report on the Police Administration, Delhi Province.* Rf. No. 228, P IV (26), General, Part 111. D.C. Office file.
2. *Ibid.*
3. *Ibid.*
4. *Ibid.*
5. *Ibid.*

6. *Ibid.*
7. *Ibid.*
8. *Ibid.*
9. *Ibid.*
10. Police Report, *ibid.*
11. *Ibid.*
12. *Ibid.*
13. See and interpret the statistics given in the police report, *ibid.*
14. *Ibid.*
15. *Ibid.*
16. *Ibid.*
17. *Ibid.*
18. Programme of events for 7th March, 1946, F/No. 6/13/46, X.B., CID, Confidential, Part B.
19. *Ibid.*
20. *Ibid.*
21. *Ibid.*
22. *Ibid.*
23. *Ibid.*
24. The Police Report, *ibid.*
25. F. No. 60/1946-B, and F. No. 6/13/46.
26. Dy. Sect. Home Dept. to C.P. of Delhi 60/1946/B, Confidential.
27. *Ibid.* W.D. Robinson to Chief Commissioner, Delhi.
28. FIR No. 221, dated 7.3.46, Police Station Kotwali, from Police Report.
29. *Ibid.*
30. Christie to the Secretary, Government of India, F. No. 60/1946/B.
31. *Ibid.*
32. Christie to Prior, Government of India, F. No. 62/46, B, Confidential.
33. *Ibid.*
34. *Ibid.*
35. *Ibid.*
36. Baldev Singh to the Secretary, Government of India, F. No. 62/46/B, Confidential.

37 *Ibid.*
38. FIR No. 168, dated 20.5.1946, Police Report, 1946, *ibid.*
39. *Ibid.*
40. *Ibid.*
41. Christie to Porter, F.No. 113/46, Confidential, Part B, CCO files.
42. *Ibid.*
43. *Ibid.*
44. *Ibid.*
45. *Ibid.*
46. Christie to Porter, F.No. 113/46, Confidential, Part B, CCO files.
47. W.D. Robinson's telephone message, F.No. 113/46-C.
48. *Ibid.*
49. *Ibid.*
50. *Ibid.*
51. *Ibid.*
52. A.E. Porter to Christie, *ibid.*
53. *Ibid.*
54. *Ibid.*
55. *Ibid.*
56. Randhawa's confidenatial letter, *ibid.*
57. *Ibid.*
58. *Ibid.*
58. *Ibid.*

2

CONTROVERSIAL RELIGIOUS SITES

Communalism is not religion. But this proposition is not entirely true as communal feeling is fed by 'religious sentiments'. When religious sentiment of a community is stimulated to an 'end' and when the 'end' is something other than religious, the society finds itself trapped in the communal net. In other words, when religion is politicized for political, economic or other ends, communalism emerges. It is, however, altogether a different matter that politics of religion is always harmful for smooth functioning of the state as also the society and economy.

In the pre-independence Indian society, 'religion' and 'religious sites' became synonymous. The abuse of 'religious site', therefore, meant the abuse of religion itself. In this background, the 'abusing of such sites' became a political and strategic instrument and weapon for the brokers of religion to stimulate the religious sentiments and to make innocent mind stained in communal colour. Once this was done, it became very easy to mobilize the masses under their political banner to serve their interests which was bound to be poisonous for social health. One thing is quite clear here is that communalism is not a 'false consciousness' and 'negative consciousness' as many modern historians believe, but it is a 'stimulated' and 'imposed' consciousness under the cover of which lies the 'innocent mind'. This means communal mind may be secularized only by dissolving the 'imposed' consciousness. In other words it would be erroneous, to find out the 'structural' basis of communalism.

This approach to communalize the human mind may be witnessed in 1947-Delhi. This was evident from 'Tughlak Road incident'[1] in December 1946. This incident was regarded as 'very serious' by Ahmad Saeed, President, Jamiat-ulama, Delhi.[2] The story goes as:[3] There existed a small village near 'Dhaula Well' (now known as Dhaula Kuan) situated in New Delhi. Formerly this village was known as Moti Bagh, but unfortunately, the representation of Saeed tells, its name had been converted into "Mochi Bagh". This village was constituted by Hindus, Muslims and a few Sikh families with one Mandir for Hindus, one Gurudwara for Sikhs and one mosque for Muslims without any roof. The Muslims of the village wanted to build a roof on the mosque but it was objected by the Mahant of the Gurudwara on the ground[4] that the proximity of the Masjid to the Gurudwara will constitute a perennial source of strife'. The Muslims of the village also sent a deputation to the Hindu inhabitants regarding the construction and Ahmad Saeed concluded that Hindus were not objecting. But the obstacles to the construction created by the Mahant of the Gurudwara gradually resulted in tension between the two communities.

The Resident Magistrate, New Delhi, Atma Prakash Bagai, investigated the site and submitted his report.[5] He had altogether a different story. He described it in terms of land dispute.[6] The land in dispute was situated in Abadi Den Bagh Mohalla which covered an area of about a *Maria*. It was enclosed by *pakka* walls, 6/7 feet in height towards north and west. There was a vacant space beyond the walls. The south and west of the alleged encroachment were occupied by *kaccha* houses of some Muslim inhabitants, Jahangir and Allah respectively. The land in dispute which was being used for offering Namaz seemed to have been in the 'unauthorized possession' of the Muslims of Bagh Mochi for a few years. The land according to the report, belonged to the Delhi Improvement Trust. Till February 1947, there existed no superstructure but Muslims wanted to build that with a view to converting it into a full-fledged mosque. The Delhi Improvement Trust should have filed an ejection suit against the Muslims and Atma Prakash Bagai suggested that an injunction order prohibiting them could be secured against the construction of any superstructure on the existing walls till the decision on the case.

After observing the above-mentioned approach of the concerned authorities, the Muslims took a strong line and wrote to Christie, the Chief Commissioner, Delhi.[7] Their argument ran as follows:

(a) *that there was only one old mosque in the village.* In contrast, a temple had been constructed outside the village and also there was a Gurudwara outside the village, but the mosque was inside the village;

(b) that *Hindus [caste Hindus] had associated themselves with the Sikhs* and *chamars* etc., and "are always after us". *They blow the "sankhs at the time of our prayers";*

(c) That the Hindus put every kind of hindrance in the discharge of religious functions of the Muslims. On 26th January 1947 *they got 5 Muslims arrested under section 452/148 falsely.* About a fortnight earlier they got arrested one man by falsely implicating him in a case.

(d) *That the Hindus had thrown stones on the mosque at the prayer time on the evening of the 'Holi' festival* and 11 Muslims along with 14 Hindus had been arrested.

On these grounds the Muslims demanded 'sympathy' from the Chief Commissioner, Delhi. But the administration agreed to follow the line suggested by the Resident Magistrate.[8]

The modality of communalizing the mind becomes very clear from the dispute stated above. First, a site was chosen. It was then given a 'religious colour'. The process was gradual. The case originally was of land grabbing, as is clear from the Resident Magistrate's reports. A Muslim religiosity was imposed upon it and was made antagonistic to the Sikh community. The Sikh community later joined hands with the Hindu community and a 'Namaz-Sankh' controversy was created. To this, the traditional Hindu-Sikh antagonism against Muslims was revived and some problems of 'Holi' festival were also added to it. Thus communalism was 'constructed' not by the colonial government itself but by the 'politics of religion' played by concerned interests.

A similar controversy was raised by the Muslims of Kishanganj.[9] Here, a *Chabutra,* which had the appearance of a mosque, was created by Muslims of Kishanganj between a well and a graveyard in front of the terminal tax post, on land handed over to Delhi Administration by canal authorities in connection with the Trust's west Jamuna canal closure scheme. No permission of the Trust was taken,[10] and purely as a matter of grace, Le Bailly, then Officiating Chairman, Delhi Improvement Trust, directed the structures to be demarcated and walled off.[11] It was decided by the Board to enclose the well and the grave and the Central Public Works Department were authorized to carry out the work.[12]

The Muslims extended their encroachment much beyond the original demarcation, which was made by the land officer in consultation with persons apparently in-charge of the so-called mosque. A wall was built on the encroached sites and they were planning to erect a superstructure over it so that the graveyard could not be taken back.[13] The local inhabitants were trying their best to give it a communal colour. Though the communal elements of Kishanganj village were not successful in creating a Hindu-Muslim tension due to the speedy action of the administrators concerned they, all the same, tried their best to do so.

But the process can best be explained by Ram Lila Ground incident[14] where it was reported that the Hindus of the area had demolished a mosque and had built a temple there. The story runs as follows: An old temple idol of *Shri Hanumanji* had been recovered on the northern side of Ram Lila Ground. Then the Hindus of the area demolished a mosque and started building a temple, as evident from a representation to the Government of India.[15] But D.I.G. Police who investigated the site reported that "there is at present no sign of a mosque and the site has been handed over to the President, Ram Lila Committee under the orders of the District Magistrate, Delhi". The Chief Commissioner and Government of India were informed of the above position. The Land and Development Officer of New Delhi was also made aware of the problem.

The Land and Development Officer in his letter16 informed that "temples in New Delhi have been leased to Shri Ram Sanatan Dharam Sabha, a body recognized by the government".[17] The Land and Development Officer, in a subsequent letter,[18] had pointed out that the construction work of the temple had been started and requested that the president of the Ram Lila Committee be directed to apply for necessary permission before proceeding with the construction of the structure.

The two Special Magistrates, Mushtaq Ahmad and Padam Chand, who visited the site of the proposed site along with D.S.P. and S.H.O., Faiz Bazar Police Station, were of the opinion that the place was an old temple of Hanumanji with pindis of Shiva. In view of this they suggested[19] it should be handed over to Lala Shri Ram, Bar-at-law, who was President of Gauri Shankar Temple. The D.S.P. city along with T. Singh, S.P., also supported the proposal and it was agreed to by Randhawa, the D.S.P.

In a subsequent report, the two magistrates stated that some miscreants were trying to create trouble and that it was likely to continue unless steps were taken to make full use of the site. They, therefore, suggested that the place be used for educational purposes and that Lala Shri Ram, who was in possession of the site and who was also the president of the Happy School Society be asked to use the site for construction of Happy School and the temple should also be maintained in its present state by the above society which was a registered body.[20] Thus the foregoing report meant a change in their earlier report to the extent that the site was to be handed over to Lala Shri Ram as president of Happy School Society.[21] It also meant that instead of handing over the site to the Hindus, it should be handed over to a society which was managed jointly by the Hindus and the Muslims.[22]

In this connection, the City Magistrate received a verbal complaint by Abdul Sattar,[23] a member of the Mosque Restoration Committee that a temple was being built on the site of an alleged mosque in *Takiya* called *Daroga ji* outside the Turkman Gate adjacent to the Ram Lila Ground. On this, the City Magistrate inspected the site and found that the construction of a temple was in progress. The construction of the temple was stopped after complaint which was taken seriously by Lala Shri Ram who wrote[24] to the concerned officers:

(1) that the site in Ram Lila Ground known as Temple of Hanumanji was handed over to me for management;

(2) that in view of the scorching heat of these days, a few kind donors commenced to build a small room, close to the temple, to provide shade and shelter to the pujari and others who come either for worship or for their morning exercise;

(3) that about a week ago, when I was out of station, the City Magistrate, at a mere report of a few communal minded Muslims, ordered the construction to be stopped;

(4) that the action taken by the City Magistrate was uncalled for and is not justifiable as per report of the D.S.P. City, S.P. City and two Special Magistrates who had inspected the spot;

(5) that the *Takiya* to which these few communal minded Muslims refer is a different site altogether and is about two furlongs distance from this and thus they are making false reports and false allegations. The *Takiya* and the graveyard are still lying intact;

(6) that there is no objection to the temple site being used for the construction of an educational institution and I have no objection if it is utilized for the construction of the Happy School as suggested by the City Magistrate, but the temple should be maintained side by side.

The proposed building being a social institution like school or sarai it was supported by the Muslims, but they were no longer agreeable to the construction of Hanuman Mandir. The City Magistrate, therefore, suggested that with consultation and approval of Mehar Chanda Khanna, Convener of the Mosque Restoration Committee, the site might be handed over to Shri Padam Chand, the founder of the Happy School. But no final action was taken and the problem was referred to and included in the list of disputed sites.

So, whatever may be the outcome, one point is crystal clear that this issue, along with other issues of similar nature, possessed the required potential to push Delhi into a 'communal trap' which meant a 'vertical' split of the society into few blocks with their specific leadership and ideology with divisive tendencies. Clearly, it was against the interest of the nation but at the same time favourable to the sectarian leadership and their political benefactors.

The matter was very serious and a meeting of the Mosque Restoration Subcommittee was held with Maulana Abul Kalam Azad in the chair to examine cases in which the character of certain structures was disputed to be either a mosque or a temple. Though it is true that in most of the cases satisfactory settlements between the communities had been arrived at, the preponderance and abundance of such cases in the year of our proposed study suggests that they contributed a lot in communalizing the social and political life of Delhi. The level of communalization was very high as there were many disputed sites which needed a serious attention. From the reports available to us the procedure of recorded and oral evidences were deliberately avoided was this might have not only protracted the proceedings but might have also engendered avoidable partisan controversy.[25] Thus we are handicapped due to absence of reliable facts. But we may still be able to have an idea of the extent of the public controversy on the controversial sites and the scope of the social tension at least by citing some cases and the knowledge available about them.

[A] Mosque of Takya, outside Turkman Gate, Ram Lila Ground, Police Station, Faiz Bazar:[26] Neither Wilson's Survey nor the Municipal House Tax Register had any entry about the existence of a mosque at the disputed site. It appears that in 1934, the Superintendent of Land and Development Office observed that a part of the city wall had been white-washed and that close to this section there were rough indications of a grave. The grave was allowed to continue but there was no formal recognition of the fact by way of execution of a lease

by the Land and Development Officer in favour of the Sunni Majlis-e-Ausaf or any other registered body. Soon after the disturbances in October 1947, a report was made that an idol of Hanuman ji had been discovered at the time of digging the platform of the monument.

The Deputy Commissioner appointed a committee of three persons to investigate the rival claims of the communities. Lala Padma Chand and Mushtaq Ahmad were members of the committee. The committee reported that no mosque at any time existed on the site. The Deputy Commissioner subsequently handed over the site at about the same time accompanied by Abdul Sattar. The latter pointed out that certain places which he thought were parts of a mosque, the City Magistrate could not find traces of any such structure. The Superintendent of Police, Jagannath had served for over ten years in Delhi and said that there was no mosque at the disputed site. All the officers were equally clear that there was no temple on this site either. Possibly there existed only a grave at the disputed site which was demolished during the disturbances and that certain Hindus took advantage of confusion to install an idol of Hanuman. The disputed site was therefore neither a mosque nor a mandir but an illegal and unauthorized encroachment.

[B] *Mosque Haju Aki Jan, Katra Bhagat, Bazar Ghanta-Ghar Police Station, and Kotwali:*[27] In Wilson's Survey of 1910-11, this place is shown as a mosque. The corresponding Municipal House Tax Register number is 175. A sum of Rs. 426-14-0 is shown as arrears on account of house tax for shops attached to the mosque. The dues are regarded payable by the Mutwali of the mosque, c/o Abdul Haq of Haji Ali Ahmad Jan of

Delhi. The Hindus claimed that a temple stood on the site at one time and that the idols now installed were recovered from beneath the floor of the mosque. This in itself was an indirect admission of the fact that a mosque existed on the site. The claim put forward by the Hindus thus appears to be spurious.

[C] *A Mosque under Police Station, Kotwali:*[28] Neither Wilson's Survey nor the Municipal House Tax Register contains any entry about the existence of a mosque at the disputed site. None of the people of the locality confirmed that a mosque or a temple existed at the site. Though it appears from the enquiries made that some railway coolies made an encroachment on the municipal land and started an *Akhara*. Later a tin shed was laid. The Municipal Committee issued several notices for removing the encroachment but did not act firmly enough. The temple which existed there was of recent origin and was obviously erected after the disturbances. The real position at the place of dispute was that there was no mosque at the site and the construction of the temple was illegal and unauthorized.

[D] *Mosque Rajpur Road, Outside Bungalow No. 10, Police Station, Civil Lines:*[29] It appears that at one time there was a grave at the site and subsequently in 1929 one Kallen alias Jumma Khan started living there. Gradually he began to encroach upon a compound of the adjoining building. The Delhi Municipal Committee brought a notice/suit against him in 1937. The court accepted the existence of a grave and a 'hut' on the site and accordingly decided against the Municipal Committee. The existence of a mosque was neither claimed by the parties nor accepted by the court. Thereafter Jumma Khan made a further encroachment and started a piao by placing pitchers of water over the parapet wall of the culvert adjoining the hut. After Jumma Khan's death in 1946, his relatives remained in possession till the disturbances in 1947. But in the same year possession was taken away by one Radhe Sham who installed some idols. The grave as well as the hut were removed during the disturbances. Thus it is clear that neither a temple nor a hut existed at the disputed site.

[E] *Mosque Takia Bela Road, Opposite Octroi Post, Civil Lines, Police Station:*[30] In 1923, one Maulavi Abdul Rahim encroached upon this land and was prosecuted by the Notified Area Committee. He admitted the error and did not express any inclination to execute lease for the site encroached upon. In 1946, one of his successors Mohammad Hussain submitted plans for the construction of a mosque, a hudra and a platform.

These plans were rejected by the committee in August 1946. In October 1946, he submitted a fresh plan which included the construction of kitchen and a latrine. These plans were again rejected by the committee. In the mean time one L. Amar Nath installed some idols there and the controversy started. But the fact was that neither mosque nor temple existed there.

[F] *Mosque Dhobtuwali, Ranch Kuyan Road, Police Station, Reading Road:*[31] The dispute about the character of the site was before the Civil Court. One Swami Rama Nand was in possession of the site. The case was similar to the other case, which we have already dealt with, concerned with illegal land grabbing and unauthorized construction.

From the case studies mentioned above, the symbiotic relationship between land grabbing and unauthorized construction, and the communalization of the social atmosphere became very clear. Both fed upon each other and supported each other. It is a self-driving mechanism which needed no outside support. Hindus and Muslims both used this technique in the time of disturbances for furthering their goals which meant nothing but more and more communalization of Delhi. The disputed religious sites became the most potent cause for communal flare-ups in Delhi as elsewhere in India. These were used for unauthorized occupation, residential purposes and commercial establishments. This separate and militant identity of the community in possession of the site, should be seen in the context of politics of the locality stimulated by municipal or local board elections. In the context of charged communal atmosphere of Delhi during the partition and its aftermath, the possession of the religious sites became in public eye the symbol of political victory. The Muslim sites were the places of social and political congregation easily identifiable by the police and militant Hindu organizations. The Hindu sites offered effective protection to the refugee *satsangs*, apart from being areas of social congregation. In the absence, of definite registered owners, these sites often became commercially attractive for speculators. In any case, they were the centres of communal discourses for the Hindus as well as Muslims charged by communal passions.

REFERENCES

1. H.F. 180/1947, D.C. Office.
2. Ahmad Saeed to the Deputy Commissioner, *ibid.*
3. *Ibid.*
4. The copy of SHO Tughlaq Road's report, dated 17 December 1946, *ibid.*

5. *Ibid.*
6. *Ibid.*
7. *Ibid.*, dated 21 June 1947.
8. *Ibid.*
9. Home File No. 181/1947, D.C. Office.
10. *Ibid.*
11. *Ibid.*
12. *Ibid.*
13. *Ibid.*
14. H.F No. 184/1947, D.C. Office.
15. *Ibid.*
16. *Ibid.*
17. *Ibid.*
18. *Ibid.*
19. *Ibid.*
20. *Ibid.*
21. *Ibid.*
22. *Ibid.*
23. *Ibid.*
24. *Ibid.*
25. *Ibid.*
26. *Ibid.*
27. *Ibid.*
28. *Ibid.*
29. *Ibid.*
30. *Ibid.*
31. *Ibid.*

3

PRESS

The 'making of communal riots' is a process in which many factors interact with one another resulting in a somewhat recognizable structure with a 'soft solidity' at the core and 'viscous fluidity' at the periphery. This structure, due to its inherent characteristic as is stated above, continued to evolve. In other words, communalism means a structured value system and ideology in a 'fused' state. Press, community consciousness, communal organizations, government policies, political parties, economic fluctuations and other elements help different social identities to 'assert'. The 'magnitude' of these assertions depends upon the 'differential' interaction of the above-mentioned variables in the process of evolution of communal consciousness.

Press, posters and other popular publications sometimes start playing the role of the mouthpiece of different communities and communal organizations. The high-pitched campaign carried out through these media helped in raising the communal fever to even higher level. Communalism, on its part, feeds on popular media. The role of administration or state in these circumstances becomes one of the opposition, which provides the leverage to their unexpected growth. Hence, emerges a tri-polar relationship between communalism and media, media and administration and administration and communalism, a self-sustained process. If one is successful in analyzing the relationship between media and administration, the level of communal fever can also be estimated over time with careful calculation of 'time-gap' between propagation of 'ideology' and administrative 'reaction'.

Before coming to the proposed year of study, it may be helpful to have a brief glance over administrative attitude towards the press in 1946. That the press played a powerful role is evident from the reply of Chief Commissioner of Delhi to the Government of India for the import of 'recent' disturbances of Bombay, Calcutta, Karachi, and Madras to Delhi.[1] In reply, wrote Christie,[2] '... the principal cause of these disorders is the press which deliberately distorts and magnifies events or alternatively omits important points.... Press advisory committees are nearly all in the hands of the worst offenders. Inflammatory speeches by politicians, many of them are amongst the leaders of their parties are source of trouble'. The principal cause of the events of 7th March disorders "is unquestionably the press — both newspapers and books.... In order to advance the interests of their particular parties, and in case of lesser newspapers to secure better sales, they even manufacture news at times and often grossly exaggerate unimportant events whichare twisted in the light favourable to them".[3] For example, on the occasion of the Victory Day Celebrations while the big capital was made out of the strong criticism leveled against the decision of the Delhi Municipality to permit the illumination of municipal buildings, no mention was made of the fact that this was being done at government and not municipal expense.[4]

Here, in this context, one may analyse the cartoons controversy[5] of *Dawn,* a Muslim League paper printed in Delhi, the issue being published on 8th and 10th of November. The first cartoon of 8th November suggests that 'the North-West India (the Muslim majority zone) is asleep while the Hindu lion has seated itself with the corpses of Bihar Muslims'[6] and the second cartoon of 10th November suggests that 'the same area remains unmoved contending itself by sending two tiny medical missions when something more is wanted'.[7] These two cartoons treated by the Punjab Government as the "most provocative"[8] and the Chief Commissioner of Delhi was requested by the Punjab Government to "warn the editor of the *Dawn*"[9] against printing such cartoons.

There is still another example, again from the *Dawn*[10], which was seriously scanned by the officials. Here it would be very meaningful if one quotes few passages from the issue of 25th November 1946. Reporting on Rohtak situation, the newspaper maintained:[11]

[A]"A particular community has been busy training its rank and file since long. The use of *lathi* and other lethal weapons was being taught at several places in the town. The activities of Rashtriya Swayam Sewak Sangh were in full swing. The I.N.A. men, armed deserters of the Indian Army and demobilized soldiers of the army were taking part in such preparations.

Certain government servants, including a police official were often reported to be taking keen interest in the activities of the R.S.S."[12]

[B] "Headed by the President of a well known communal body, who is also a doctor, they lodged a false report with the police that they had purchased some oranges and some bananas from a fruit seller which were later found to be poisoned. It is however obvious that if these fruits were found to be poisoned, it must have been the mischief of the Dr. President".[13]

[C] "Reports of very alarming nature are being received from rural areas that forcible conversion is going on. The local authorities who failed to take preventive measures and are conniving at these widespread crimes are cleverly trying to throw the whole blame at the doors of the victims themselves".[14]

What is important here is not that the publication but its timing and structure of the language. It was not just an accident that Paharganju riots and the cartoons already mentioned came into the being almost simultaneously. It is difficult to move far away from the conclusion that 'sponsoring' of cartoons had its direct link with the Paharganj riot. Again the articles published in Rohtak on communal trouble in *Dawn* on 25th November was meant, one may conclude, to maintain the waning communal fever above the 'critical threshold'. If we examine the given 'structure' of the Rohtak report, the clubbing of R.S.S., the I.N.A., the police, and the 'poisoning and conversion' into a single whole, it simply meant to render the security of the Muslim community totally endangered and to jeopardize their existence in 'Hindu Delhi', or for that matter in the 'Hindustan'. The inflammatory use of the media, therefore, perpetuated the communal imagination to the highest point, having all the required potential to erupt into volcanic riot.

It becomes here important to examine the administrators' reaction to the complaint against these cartoons and the 'questionable reports; in the *Dawn.* W. Christie, the Chief Commissioner, was of the opinion that "security of Rs. 3,000/- being demanded from the keeper of *Dawn* and from the publisher of *Dawn* specifically because of these two cartoons but also in view of the other provocative articles and the items which have appeared in it during recent months".[15] Porter was to agree with the solution.[16] The administration's measure was mild and the Dawn was allowed to continue its rabid communal propaganda. Once again, one can easily surmise that the administrators were not very serious of the otherwise very dangerous consequences. It was certainly a significant administrative lapse.

There were some feasible alternatives for the administration. The bureaucracy had itself suggested three measures[17] after the Victory Day Celebration incidents. These were: (a) by speedy action against offending newspapers and presses where they are printed, i.e., demanding securities under the Indian Press (Emergency Powers) Act, 1931. The editors and publishers of newspapers and keepers of their presses should also be prosecuted under any other Acts, if contravened';[18] (b) 'by imposing pre-censorship on local newspapers, or a section thereof, in grave emergencies, when disturbances of public peace have taken place or are apprehended'[19] ... and 'side by side with the pre-censorship orders against the local press, restriction under section 5 of the Indian Telegraph Act, 1885 should also be imposed on outgoing telegrams which are very numerous';[20] and (c) 'by keeping in existence and proper functioning a consultative body of responsible editors of local papers to exercise *friendly restraint* on the press'.

One more problem in this regard was the dealing with the 'objectionable books' which had been published in fairly large numbers during 1946 and 47, especially in Indian languages. Under section 9 of the Press and Registration of Books Act, 1867, the keepers of presses were required to deliver one copy of each book printed by them at the office of the District Magistrate within one month of its publication.[21] Within this period, almost all copies of an objectionable book were sold. Often the keepers of the presses did not deliver copies of such books at all and there was no means at the disposal of the District Magistrate to detect the omission unless the book was brought to his notice.

To meet this problem, three precautionary measures were suggested:[22] (a) that the said section 9 be amended; (b) a capable Inspectorate of Presses be organized to inspect all presses periodically; and (c) in the period of emergency, keepers of presses in general or a section thereof be required to submit books on any particular subject proposed to be printed by them for scrutiny before publication. Bailly, the S.S.P. of Delhi, admits that the proposals given were likely to be described as an 'interference with the freedom of press', but in view of the possible threats to the public peace they appear to be most essential".[23] But the rationality of Bailly's argument failed to attract the imagination of other British administrators, as has already been hinted.

The administrative problems of 1946 are now understandable and so the scope of the possibility of their solution. It is under this background, the position of press vis-a-vis communal position and the changing temper of the public opinion and administrative inaction during 1947 may be beneficial to our study.

On the communal front, the period between mid December 1946 to the first half of January 1947 was almost peaceful.[24] The headlines of the newspapers are concerned with other issues than communal. For example, the proceedings of the Constituent Assembly were prominently featured in the press and satisfaction expressed in a majority of the newspapers on the decision of the Constituent Assembly to postpone final consideration of the resolution of the objectives of that body.[25] The press severely criticized the French aggression in Indo-China, the U.S. policy in China and other affairs[26] not very important from the communal point of view. Again, the Congress' acceptance of His Majesty's Government's statement of 6th December 1946 was welcomed by the nationalist press, which, however made it clear that the interests of Assam and NW Frontier Province, and of the Sikh and Hindu minorities in Bengal and the Punjab should be fully safeguarded.[27] The Muslim League papers led by *Dawn* on the other hand, described the Congress resolution ambiguous and half-hearted acceptance of the British Government statement.[28]

Due to the relative communal peace, the rumour spreading centre and the propaganda machinery of different communities and their mouthpieces, the newspapers, raised their 'pitch' and 'playground'. But even on this higher plane latent communalization can be discerned in their division in terms of the "nationalist newspapers and Muslim League's papers; criticizing and counter-criticizing one another. The administrators showed no seriousness in the matter and decided merely to keep on the 'vigil'."[29]

But the situation gradually became increasingly more tense between the second half of January and the first half of February 1947.[30] The events in Punjab and the meeting of the Working Committee of the Muslim League at Karachi were the main features.[11] The Punjab Government's decision to ban the Rashtriya Swayam Sewak Sangh and the Muslim National Guards came as a sudden surprise and caused much excitement.[32] The subsequent withdrawal of the ban was another surprise but much of the tension remained in the political atmosphere.[33] It however came at a very crucial moment for the League which had been weakened by internal dissensions and was in danger of becoming moribund.[34]

Press twisted the news. The Muslim press strongly criticized[35] the action of Punjab Government in banning the Muslim National Guards and not the R.S.S. and arresting the Muslim League leaders and the *Dawn* in particular made much capital out of these events which it had "obviously exaggerated for its own purpose".[36] The Punjab Government issued a ban against the paper entering that province.[37] The *Dawn* had been making much of the demonstrations in the Punjab, as there was a vast difference between its account and those contained in the Punjab Government communiques,[38] but the government did not think it advisable to ban the communal paper in Delhi as had been done by the Punjab Government.

This trend continued in the second half of February and the first half of March.[39] The events of the period were (a) termination of Muslim League's civil disobedience movement in Punjab, and (b) the resignation of the Punjab premier and his government.[40] Punjab Day was observed by the Delhi Muslim League on 24th February with a large meeting followed by the usual procession which moved round the city shouting 'objectionable' slogans. The seriousness of the matter was reflected from the understanding of Christie, when he evaluated the situation. 'The serious and widespread disturbances in the Punjab, following the resignation of the Union Ministry have gravely agitated people of all classes and communities, and communal feeling in Delhi, which had shown a welcome improvement in previous weeks have again deteriorated seriously". The scarcity of news contained in official communiques issued by the Punjab authorities encouraged the spreading of 'wild rumours. Publication of 'garbled' and 'exaggerated' reports added to it.[41] In this background, 'Anti-Pakistan Day' was celebrated which ignited the communal feelings but 'without any serious incident' which helped the British administrators to conclude that the event needed no further discussions.[42]

Events in the Punjab were very prominently featured in all sections of the press "without restraint desirable or promised".[43] The government was not totally inactive to this front. There was a move to include newspapers to the "Censorship List".[44] The reasons,[45] however, were given as: (a) to curb left wing parties' activities and (b) to stop government's officials writing in newspapers and thus to stop the 'administrative leakages'. The papers which were suggested to be scrutinized regularly included:[46]

1. *The Hindustan Times,* New Delhi.
2. *The Dawn,* Faiz Bazaar Road, Delhi.

3. *The National Call,* Mori Gate, Delhi.
4. *The Janata Weekly,* Connaught Place, New Delhi.
5. *The Daily Tej,* Naya Bazaar, Delhi.
6. *The Riyasat,* Charkhewalan, Chawri Bazaar, Delhi.
7. *The Ansari.*
8. *The Anjam.*
9. *The Payam.*
10. *The Watch.*
11. *The Swarajya.*

But, the Home Department was not very enthusiastic about it. In the second half of March 1947 and till the end of the second half of April,[47] the communal situation was very serious. Press played a very important role in 'magnifying' it. Refugees from Punjab brought harrowing tales of atrocities and accounts of communal violence in the press, particularly those from the special correspondents of the various papers, had a very bad effect on the morale of the people.[48] The determination of the Muslim League to celebrate Pakistan Day on 23rd March made the situation even worse. The Sikhs had already begun parading about the city in jeeps and lorries armed with their large kirpans.[49] A regrettable feature was that the public of Delhi followed the example of Punjab in alleging communalism amongst the police,[50] and press had a definite role in it. The complaints by Muslims were mainly against Sikh police officers than their Hindu counterparts,[51] and Sikhs, on the other hand, complained against Muslim police officers. Again, the serious communal disturbances in the rural area of Gurgaon had caused a good deal of alarm among the southern portion of the district. Press had definitely played a crucial role in the fanning of communal wind and the government felt it necessary to take action against a number of papers. Material published in the *Statesman, Hindustan Times, Dawn* and *National Call* were referred to the Central Press Advisory Committee.[52] A pre-censorship order was issued as regards the communal news, relating to Delhi.[53] Christie emphasized that some action had also to be taken against the press apart from a pre-censorship order, passed against a Urdu Daily called Swarajya.Thus the administrative clamping was tightened and it was tried to make the press more responsive.

The clamping down of the press was however given priority on the last quarter of the year. In October, pre-censorship orders under Section 4(b) of the Press (Special) Powers No. 2) Ordinance, 1947 were served on the editors, printers and publishers of *Dawn, Hindu Outlook, Jung, Wahadat, Alamah, Naya Daur, Aj* and Baljit. The editor of *Aj* was warned for publishing objectionable material regarding communal riots.[55] The Chief Commissioner, Delhi, demanded security of Rs 3,000/- from the publisher of *Dawn*; Rs. 1,000/- from the publisher of *Aj* and Rs 500/- each from the publishers of *Jung, Wahadat, Alaman, Baljit, Jamhoor* and *Panth* under Section 7(3) of the Indian Press Act, 1931.[56] He also ordered forfeiture of security of Rs 500/- deposited by the publisher of *Naya Daur* in compliance with the District Magistrate's order under Section 7(1) of the Indian Press Act, 1931.[57] Separate proposals for appointment of special inspectorate staff were again sent.[58]

In the next week,[59] the Chief Commissioner of Delhi had prohibited the publication of the Urdu Daily *Sangram* for a period of one month under Punjab Public Safety Act, 1947.[60] The Chief Commissioner demanded a security of Rs. 2,000/- under Section 7(3) of the Indian Press Emergency Powers Act, 1931 from the publisher of the English weekly *Hindu Outlook* for publishing an objectionable article entitled "Feature of Indian Union" in its issue of 9th September 1947.[61] Warnings were issued to the editors of *Tej, Milap* and *Aj* for publishing lurid accounts of communal disturbances in West Punjab.[62]

Actions were also taken against unauthorized newssheets, pamphlets and posters. An Urdu pamphlet entitled, "How far is it true that the present policy of the Government is detrimental to the interests of the Hindus", issued by Gulab Singh, Babu Ram and Hazari Lal was found in circulation.[63] The pamphlet was found objectionable and D.I.G. of Police had been asked to register a case under Section 18 of the Indian Press (Emergency) Act. The Gupta Printing Works where the pamphlet was published was searched and two copies of the pamphlet and the original manuscript were recovered.[64]

A hand-written poster entitled "Boycott the Property of Pakistan" warning the Hindus of the risks in purchasing the property from Muslim refugees was found in circulation.[65] The C.I.D. could not trace the publisher.

An Urdu hand-bill entitled "Mera Jehad" advocating economic boycott of non-Muslims by Muslims was found in circulation. The Rajaji Press, where it was published, was searched but nothing incriminating was discovered.

A poster in Gurumukhi entitled "Pran Patra"[66] was published by Ranjit Singh, resident of Ghaziabad in U.P., and was circulated in Delhi. This poster was found highly objectionable.

Two Urdu posters entitled "Delhi ki Halchal or Hindu-Muslim Riots" were issued by Master Naider Singh Bechain and printed at the press known as the Alia Press, Bazar Sita Ram, Delhi.[67] The contents of both the pamphlets were found harmful to public health. Two more posters of the same category entitled "Massacre in Kadia" were issued by Ahmadias of Kadian and printed at the Civil and Militia Press, Karachi.[68] The C.I.D. took action against them.

An Urdu poster entitled "Kashmir in Danger" had been given by one Krishna Kumar, Editor of *Daily Pratap* residing at 10 Punch Kuina Road for publication in Gupta Printing Press, Delhi, in the jurisdiction of Police Station Kotwali, under the signature of Major Romesh and Major Chain Singh. Again the contents of the poster were objectionable which came under the purview of Section 18 of Press (Emergency Powers) Act, in case published and circulated.

The Chief Commissioner of Delhi had under Section 19 of the Indian Press (Emergency Powers) Act declared to be forfeited all copies of the booklet in Hindi entitled *"Delhi kee Dhuwavan Dhar"* (conflagration in Delhi) written by Brahma Datta Sharma, published by Jagdish Chander Sharma, Book Seller, Nai Sarak, Delhi and printed by Sugan Chand at the Dhara Press, Dariba Kalan, Delhi.[69] The Chief Commissioner also demanded security of Rs. 500/- from the keeper of Dhara Press under Section 33 of the aforesaid Act for printing this objectionable leaflet.

Under Section 19 of the India Press (Emergency Powers) Act, 1931, the Chief Commissioner declared to be forfeited to the Dominion of India all copies of the following pamphlets:[70] (i) *"Qadian"* written by Amir-ul-Mominin, printed at Civil and Military Press, Karachi; (ii) *"Qadian ki Khunrez Jung"* written by Hazrat Amir-ul-Mominin, printed at Civil and Military Press, Karachi.

The Chief Commissioner, Delhi, under Section 19 of Indian Press Act 1931 had declared to be forfeited to His Majesty all copies of the booklet in English entitled "The Greatest Betrayal" written by Chaudhari Rahmat Ali published by the Pakistan Liberation Movement, 16 Montague Road, Cambridge, England.[71]

What is noticeable from the above description is that the administration suddenly, from September became more responsible. The newspapers, popular press, posters and pamphlets, the sources of rumour, the elements having the potential to create communal frenzy and blood-shed, were properly scrutinized after independence in August. The withdrawn "imperial army" of British crown, it seems, proved good, at least in case of reestablishing peace and order, obviously after September riots.

REFERENCES

1. H.F. 180/1947. D.C. Office.
2. Ahmad Saeed to the Deputy Commissioner, *ibid.*
3. *Ibid.*
4. The copy of S.H.O. Tughlaq Road's report, dated 17 December 1946, *ibid.*
5. *Dawn,* 8th and 10th November 1946.
6. *Ibid.* 8th November 1946.
7. *Dawn,* 10th November 1946.
8. *Ibid.*
9. *Ibid.*
10. Home File No. 181/1947, D.C. Office.
11. *The Dawn,* 25 November 1946.

12. *Ibid.*
13. *Ibid.*
14. *Ibid.*
15. H.F.No. 184/1947, D.C. Office.
16. *Ibid.*
17. Bailly to Christie, dated 25 March 1946, F.No. 60/1946, Part B, Confidential (Home Department).
18. *Ibid.*
19. Such orders were issued in regard to news relating to Congress disturbances, against all newspapers in 1942, and a section of Press in 1943 in regard to news relating to Gandhi's fast, *ibid.*
20. *Ibid.*
21. *Ibid.*
22. *Ibid.*
23. *Ibid.*
24. Fortnightly Reports dated 7th January 1947, F.No. 1/1947,B-Confidential.
25. *Ibid.*
26. *Ibid.*
27. *Ibid.*
28. *Ibid.*
29. *Ibid.*
30. Fortnightly Reports, dated 7th February and 19th February 1947, *ibid.*
31. *Ibid.*
32. *Ibid.*
33. *Ibid.*
34. *Ibid.*
35. *Ibid.*
36. *Ibid.*
37. *Ibid.*
38. Christie to Porter in *ibid.*
39. Fortnightly Reports, dated 4th and 19th March 1947, F.No. 1/1947 Confidential, Part B.
40. *Ibid.*
41. *Ibid.*
42. *Ibid.*

43. *Ibid.*
44. Home File No. 29/47, Part B, Confidential.
45. *Ibid.*
46. *Ibid.*
47. Fortnightly Reports, F.No. 1/1947, Part B, Confidential.
48. *Ibid.*
49. *Ibid.*
50. *Ibid.*
51. *Ibid.*
52. *Ibid.*
53. *Ibid.*
54. *Ibid.*
55. Weekly Reports ending 18th October 1947, F.No. 68/16/47.
56. *Ibid.*
57. *Ibid.*
58. *Ibid.*
59. Weekly Report ending 18th October 1947, F.No. 68/16/47.
60. *Ibid.*
61. *Ibid.*
62. *Ibid.*
63. *Ibid.*
64. *Ibid.*
65. *Ibid.*
66. Weekly Report, week ending 1st November 1947, F.No. 68/16/1947.
67. *Ibid.*
68. *Ibid.*
69. Weekly Report ending 8 November 1947, F.No. 68/16/1947.
70. Weekly Report, week ending 29 November 1947, ibid.
71. Weekly Report, week ending 13 December 1947, ibid.16/1947.

4

COMMUNAL ORGANIZATIONS

Communalism as has already been explained in the previous chapter is a process that does not mechanically correspond to a set of social factors but also has psychological and mental dimensions. It is, therefore, not a 'structure' in the 'structural sense'. Economics and politics determine the mechanical process involved in it whereas psychology and therefore ever-changing mental state, individual or collective, provide the emerging 'structure' a fluidity and flexibility. But there exists barriers between the state of "individual mind" and "collective mind". In the extreme situations, individual state of mind approaches the collective state and in this process almost every institution including schools, colleges, *panchayats,* festivals along with police and administration take communal colour. Here the social tension crosses the 'critical point' from where starts the 'communal rioting'. 'Communal riots' are, therefore, not the result of mechanized part of the process but one determined by the 'specific' state of mental fluidity; the specificity of that state is attained by changing vision of press and of public opinion through communal organizations.

The important communal organizations of Delhi in 1947 were the R.S.S., the Hindu National Guards, the Muslim National Guards, the Akali Dal, the Akal Regiment; the Sikh National Volunteer Corps, etc. In the changing political scenario, all of them tried to pose themselves as the perfect protectors of the respective community each of them represented. In the name of protecting their respective community interests, each of them started projecting the community it represented, above the composite social structure resulting into the 'cracks' in the social fabric. The society therefore started moving towards the direction where it contained only Hindus, Muslims or Sikhs as different social blocks with specific identities and thus an Indian identity, a homogeneous amalgamation of all the communities into an integrated whole were nowhere seen. This was the 'modality' according to which the 1947 Delhi was structured and thus emerged communal violence in the period concerned.

After the Paharganj riot in November 1946, the communal situation in Delhi started improving but not in the sense that the community identity melted into a national identity. The respective communal identity and consciousness remained intact. It was decided to create Hindu National Guards to protect the interests of the Hindu community.[1] The Muslim National Guards were already in existence with the membership approaching near 700.[2] Many Muslim leaders of Muslim National Guard had already started complaining that "insufficient interest is being taken in them"[3] by the Muslim population. "No parade has been held for some time, nor has there been any recent training in the use of weapons".[4] They were regarded by the government as "the most potential dangerous organization on the Muslim side at present".[5] Along with them there were about 50 *Khaksars* in Delhi but showing 'no particular activity recently' apart from holding weekly meetings.[6] The Khaksars were involved in certain cases. During that time, the R.S.S. had a strength of about 3,000 of whom all but 500 were in the urban area of Delhi and cantonment.[7] All branches of the Sangh had been performing physical exercises regularly but had no recent significant political engagement which meant that they decided to probe a defensive policy. The Azad Hind Dal, organized by the Forward Bloc had a strength only about 200 and were not showing any sign of activities in the month of December 1946 and, strangely enough, the government characterized it as a communal organization. That is to say that there existed a 'calm, a dangerous calm' having all the potential to explode any time.

But a change, however slow might be, was perceivable. In a relatively peaceful condition, the internal dissentions in the local Muslim League came to the fore with the moving of a number of no confidence motions against the President and the Secretary of, Delhi Provincial Muslim League.[8] Though the resolution was subsequently withdrawn, yet the members of opposition submitted their resignation from the Provincial Muslim League Council.[9] This inactivity and the resultant dissention in the League confirms the fact that for the existence of an organization, communal in character, it was necessary to be always in move. Otherwise it was prone to lose its edge and legitimacy for its existence.

A radical programme became for the Muslim League the cry of the time. The events of Punjab[10] and the

R.S.S. proposal to hold a big conference in Delhi[11] provided that opportunity. The Punjab Government's decision to ban the Rashtriya Swayam Sewak Sangh and the Muslim National Guards caused a good deal of excitement which was increased by the arrests of many Muslim League leaders.[12] The subsequent withdrawal of the ban,[13] a surprise step of Punjab Government, ironically increased the excitement further in the respective camps which provided an 'opportune moment' for Delhi Muslim League to overcome all its internal dissensions. The League was apprehensive that inactivity would render it virtually moribund.[14]

This strengthening of the Muslim League agitated the R.S.S. and its rejuvenation was further assisted by the banning of the R.S.S. in Punjab. The hammering by the Punjab Government dragged the Hindu right wing to the conclusion that gearing up of the organizational strength was the most necessary step. The R.S.S. therefore made the preliminary arrangements for the rally in Delhi notwithstanding the government's warning[15] to the contrary. The ban, though subsequently withdrawn and the warning against holding the rally gave rise to considerable resentment amongst 'the communally minded Hindus' who did everything in their power to get the ban removed.[16]

Due to the reasons already stated in the case of the R.S.S. and the Muslim League, the Muslim National Guards also got the opportunity and thus increased its membership[17] and therefore its own legitimacy. But it was still far from very well organized.[18]

The Muslim League activated itself by supporting the Delhi butchers strike.[19] Well-attended meetings were organized and a procession was planned jointly with the Jamiat-ul-Guresh.[20] They were responsible for an incident which occurred during Id-i-Milad celebration when they induced the processionists to stop for few hours in the middle of the city as a protest against the order which prohibited the processionists to include an elephant in their rally.[21] These activities of the Muslim League helped the All India Hindu Mahasabha to conclude that the League had been preparing for 'direct action' which resulted in a resolution warning the country for that eventuality.[22] The Hindu Mahasabha called on all sections of the people to mobilize their resources to meet this crisis so that peace of the country could be maintained.[23] It also emphasized the necessity for co-operating with other Hindu volunteer organizations such as the R.S.S. so that their help might be made available at the required time.[24] The process of community polarization which one can see and observe here, were fanned in a very planned manner by the communal organizations.

The Muslim League agitation in the Punjab helped arouse some enthusiasm amongst Muslim National Guards in Delhi, as has already been pointed out. It is, however, altogether a different thing that only 31 volunteers were sent to Punjab.[25] The important thing of the month of February was the formation of two new volunteer organizations, 'though it is not very easy to link it with Punjab affairs'. The impact of the event, however, cannot be denied, if one thinks in terms of conjectural theory. The Jatav Sabha Dal had been formed by the chamars of Shahadara and about 14 volunteers were receiving regular training.[26] A potentially more important organization was the Mazdoor Sewa Dal which had been started by the Textile Mazdoor Sangh with only 40 volunteers in the corps.[27] The author would like to bring the reader to note that both these organizations were classified as communal by the officials as a sign of their opposition against political groupings.

The enthusiasm displayed by the Muslim League over what they regarded as the successful outcome of their civil disobedience movement resulted in some sort of nervousness which forced the leaders of Muslim National Guards and Bazm-i-Pakistan to concentrate chiefly on, what they called it, 'defensive precautions' for the protection of the Muslim community.[28] Even the nationalist Muslims had been outspoken against Master Tara Singh's provocative speeches and they regarded it as the responsible factor for the rioting in the Punjab. The Hindus and Sikhs jointly demonstrated in the early stage of disturbances and offered full support in the effort of preventing the formation of a Muslim League ministry.[29]

Different non-Muslim communities in Delhi were agitated by this Punjab opium and Anti-Pakistan Day was, therefore, observed jointly by the Hindus and Sikhs of Delhi on 11th March.[30] Although considerable enthusiasm was displayed at the public meetings, the attendance was actually less than what had been expected. An 'Anti-Pakistan Council' was formed, the members of which, interestingly, were children and young and so-called irresponsible elements of the Hindu and Sikh communities including students.[31] The R.S.S., on its part, held its annual rally on 9th of March, in which one lakh of volunteers were present, of whom about half were from outside Delhi.[32] Madho Rao Golvalkar, the Sangh chief, in his speeches and subsequent private meetings gave "strict instructions" that all "outsiders" should leave Delhi without delay.[33]

The recent announcement of the British Government to hand over powers in India to Indians not later than June 1948 was partly responsible for increased activities of the Sangh.[34]

The disturbances in the Punjab had the inevitable result of igniting dangerously the communal tension in Delhi. Refugees from the Punjab brought harrowing tales of atrocities and accounts in the press, particularly those from the special correspondents of various papers. It had a bad effect on the morale of the people.[35] The determination of the Muslim League to celebrate Pakistan Day on 23rd March[36] made the environment more explosive. At the same time, the Sikhs had begun parading about the city in jeeps and lorries armed with large kirpans and trouble started when one such jeep collided with a Muslim cyclist in front of Jama Masjid.[37] Again, the serious communal disturbances in the rural area of Gurgaon caused a good deal of alarm among the villagers of the southern portion of the district,[38] and to a lesser extent the whole of Delhi. Even worse was the tendency of political leaders and press to make wild allegations, true or structured, based on violent outpourings on every possible occasion, having an adverse effect on the morale of police not any longer untouched and uninfluenced by communalism.[39]

In this situation, the members of Akali Dal became very active in the name of defending the Sikh community in Delhi[40] and took part in the observance of 'Anti-Pakistan Day' on 11th March and were closely associated with the 'Anti-Pakistan Council of Action'.[41] The organization, 'Akal Regiment' was formed during the month of March by a number of young Sikhs and two thousand volunteers were enlisted.[42] For the purpose of defending the Sikh community in Delhi the Regiment had been divided into a number of divisions, each of which had been provided with transport. The leaders of the Akal Regiment were allegedly involved in the rioting near Jama Masjid,[43] which took place on the occasion of "Pakistan Day".

The successful Muslim League agitation in Punjab gave a fillip to this organization and efforts were made to expand it. After the Punjab disturbances, the Muslim National Guards were trained in defensive measures, equipped with steel helmets, and were seen patrolling in the streets of Delhi on 'Anti-Pakistan Day' on 11th March.[44] The extremist elements of this organization along with the members of Bazm-i-Pakistan had been inciting the Muslims to "disarm the Sikhs forcibly and had been endeavoring to work up a movement to secure for the Muslims the right to carry swords.[45] They continued their propaganda against the carrying of kirpans by Sikhs.[46] Two cartoons entitled "Mohammad goes to the Mount"[47] created another source of tension and even the apology by the editor was not regarded enough by the Muslim leadership.[48] The fiery speeches of the Arya Samaj leaders only acted as 'catalyst' to the whole process.

In the mean time, the Hindu communalism was propagated by the R.S.S. and the All India Dharm Sangh under the leadership of Swami Karpatriji Maharaj. The activities of this so-called greatest Hindu leader and a saint of greatest spiritual power and his "Dharmayuddha Campaign"[49] assumed significance. This organization under the leadership of Karpatriji Maharaj following their Dharmayuddha Campaign, submitted five demands[50] to the members of the Central Government, consisted of Pandit Jawahar Lal Nehru, Sardar Patel and Dr Rajendra Prasad. The demands meant for the establishment of a Hindu India, included:

I. Cow Protection: by banning cow slaughter throughout India on religious, social, physical and economic grounds. This step was to begin in Mathura, the birthplace of Lord Krishna, *Gopal,* the protector of cows.

II. Akhand Bharat: dropping all schemes of vivisection of our 'mother land'.

III. Religion to be left independent: There should be no legislative interference in religious, socio-religious and religio-social affairs of the Hindus. In this respect only great scholars and acharyas, educated in oriental learnings, were entitled to say whether a particular matter was religious or not.

IV. Sanctity of temples to be maintained according to the age long traditions and shastric injunctions. All legislation in this respect to be dropped.

V. Adequate representation of the Sanatani Hindus on the constitution making body and all its committees.

The demands suggested the aggressive posture of this Hindu organization. The concepts of "Akhand Bharat", "the increased role of religion in state affairs", "the emphasis on shastric injunctions", "the new role of *sadhus* and *acharyas*", "the importance of oriental education", "the Sanatani Hindu representation in constitution making body", "the absolutism of cow protection", etc., had sufficient potential to make the Muslims suspicious and even antagonistic and allergic to the All-India Dharam Sangh's game plan. The Dharmayuddha Campaign meant, in such a charged atmosphere, *'Jehad'*; and the bipolarity of Hindus and

Muslims. The formation of *'dharmayuddha'* and *'jehad'* created a dangerous atmosphere which even a man with ordinary common sense could understand.

But bureaucracy had something else in mind. In a confidential letter, R.N. Banerjee suggested to the Chief Commissioner, W. Christie,[51] to "release the Swami" in order to propagate his dharmayuddha. Banerjee was aware of the after-effect of his injunction. The Swami had been arrested for breach of an order under section 144 of the Criminal Procedure Code during the session of the Assembly. Banerjee wrote[52] in his order to the Subordinate, "I am desired to say that with the termination of the session of the Assembly, the Government of India do not consider it necessary to keep these persons in jail any longer; and unless you have any strong objections, I request you to have all these persons released ... the balance of the sentence being treated as remitted". It appears that the Home Ministry under the leadership of Ballava Bhai Patel was no longer allergic to Hindu communal propaganda which found a receptive ear in India's principal executive authority.

During this period there had been the occasion when the volunteers of Akal Regiment co-operated with R.S.S.[53] and had been suspected by the bureaucracy of having been responsible for some of the attacks on Muslims during recent disturbances.[54] In the meantime, R.S.S. was chiefly occupied with the collection of money and clothes for Hindu sufferers in the Punjab.[55]

The departure of Lord Ismay, Chief of Staff of His Excellency the Viceroy, created yet another situation in its favour. The conflicting claims of the Muslims for the whole of Punjab and of the Hindus and Sikhs for the partition of that province had, therefore, created a situation where it was generally felt that as soon as an announcement was made on 2nd of June, rioting would break out on a large scale simultaneously.[56] The disturbances of Amritsar and Lahore had caused considerable alarm in Delhi.[57] Under this backdrop the younger elements, the youth wing and their organizations, of the three main communities, i.e., Hindus, Muslims and Sikhs, secretly started preparing themselves for a "savage civil war".[58] Christie wrote to Banerjee[59] that all communities had been making "secret war-like preparations". Though the general impression was that the preparations were primarily defensive in the case of each community, they were not confined "to any one community". The most dangerous possibility was the "preparations of explosives and fire arms".[60] Christie was certain that individuals were collecting firearms to 'the greatest possible extent'.[61] Banerjee decided to take no note of this warning.

But before examining the charge of preparation of respective communities, it will be good to examine the political repercussions of the 'June plan'. The Sikhs were, as a whole 'dissatisfied' with the plan as whatever happened in the event of partition of the Punjab, they would be split and consequently weakened and therefore June plan was widely condemned by them.[62] The Delhi Muslims, unhappy of living in Hindustan with Hindus, supported the plan.[63] The Khaksars, however, were bitterly opposed to the Muslim League's acceptance of a "truncated Pakistan" and showed their resentment in a very 'rowdy' manner on 9th June, when the All India Muslim League was in session in Imperial Hotel, New Delhi.[64] Their leader Allama Moshriqi who came to Delhi specifically for the demonstration was later arrested and then released by the police. On the other hand, the 'orthodox' Hindus continued their agitation against the division of India and against the Congress for having agreed to it.[65] The Communists, the Socialists and the Forward Bloc were also all opposed to the June Plan.[66] The nationalist Muslims were also critical to the plan and condemned the Muslim League for accepting the form of Pakistan which would leave "several religious, cultural and industrial centres of importance of the Muslims in Hindu hands".[67] That is to say that the supporters of the plan, i.e., Congress and Muslim League, found the opposition from the right wing Hindu, Muslim and Sikh organizations which were, in their turn, opposed to the organizations of the other antagonistic communities.

Under this very framework, the different communities of Delhi started preparations for their 'action plan'. Large number of *kirpans* (said to be 100 a day) were manufactured under license by Mohan Singh in the Central P.W.D. Factory.[68] Members of the National Volunteer Corps in New Delhi were being given target practice with an air rifle.[69] Akali leaders from the Punjab had instructed local Sikhs to collect arms legally[70] and illegally. Sikhs in Delhi, therefore, purchased jeeps, motorcycles and lorries to enable their armed *jathas* to move about rapidly.[71] Efforts were being made to organize all Sikh Volunteers Organizations to be known as Shahidi Dal.[72] There were cases in the rural areas, particularly of Hindus, being converted to Sikhism for the sole purpose of carrying them swords.[73]

The Hindus, on the other hand, under the Hindu

Mahasabha, the Council of Action for Partition of Bengal, the Young Bengali Association, the Arya Samaj, the R.S.S., the Arya Dal and the All India Dharam Sangh were contemplating a demonstration in New Delhi on 2nd June to protest against the division of India.[74] The R.S.S. was known to have collected fire fighting apparatus, and steel helmets. Daily parades and exercises were being held regularly.[75]

The moderate members of the Muslim League thought only in terms of somewhat vague defensive preparations. They were, however, collecting funds for the relief of dependents involved in any future agitation or disturbances.[76] The Muslim National Guards and the Muslim League extremists had, however, been planning a demonstration on the 2nd June to support the "Pakistan Demand" of the Muslim League.[77] They were making efforts to obtain information from the police and the C.I.D. regarding matters effecting them and also planning demonstration for 'the right to carry swords' and 'to protest against the imprisonment of Maijur-ul-Haq'.[78]

Even after such intensive communalization to this extent, the much-publicized *Khaksar* rally on July 2 and 3 failed; the meeting was attended by only five thousand Khaksars while the expectation was of 3 lakhs of Khaksar volunteers.[79] Accordingly, as previously threatened by him, Allama Mashriqi disbanded its organization. But it did not end the Khaksar activity in Delhi, and police suspected that about 800 Khaksars, sheltered in various mosques with a large concentration at the mosque of Fatehpuri, were planning to prevent the hoisting of the National Flag on the Red Fort on 15 August 1947.[80]

On 9th and 10th August, the All India Hindu

Convention was held in New Delhi under the presidentship of V.D. Savarkar where resolutions[81] were passed demanding the National Flag of India should be a "saffron coloured Hindu flag"; Hindi should be the *lingua franca* of the country; Pakistan should be made part of Hindustan. The so-called Congress policy of Muslim appeasement was criticized.

After independence, the communal tension again surcharged the city of Delhi, owing to the influx of refugees from West Punjab. Disturbances were not confined to the city alone but also spread to the rural areas. In fact, the trouble started from the rural areas and then swept over the city.[82]

Extremist Hindus and Sikhs expressed acute dissatisfaction and resentment at the government's policy of 'rehabilitating Muslims in Delhi mainly on account of failure of the Government of India to secure reciprocal arrangements and guarantee of safety for non-Muslims in Lahore and in other places in the Dominion of Pakistan and partly because Hindus and Sikhs still looked on Muslims with considerable suspicion.[83] But the nationalist Muslims, on their part, created a new organization called the "Sadaqat Committee" with a view to countering the Muslim League propaganda and bringing about cordial relations between the two major communities.[84] A meeting was held in Jama Masjid after Juma prayer on 1st October under the auspices of the Majlis-i-Ahrar and Jamayat-ul-Ulema in which Jinnah, his policy and his Pakistan were denounced[85] for their aggressive tenor.

Meanwhile the All India Hindu Mahasabha started a new propaganda. It demanded that the non-Muslims of India should be militarily trained to save the country from a sudden attack of Pakistan or any other Muslim power.[86] In furtherance of this object, meetings were held in Kishan Nagar on 6th October under the Hindu Mahasabha banner, and on 9th and 12th under the auspices of the Hindu Sahitya Samiti, Frontier Hindu-Sikh Relief Committee and Arya Yuvak Sangha.[87] It was urged here that arms licenses should be given liberally to non-Muslims.[88] Hindu Mahasabha made clear its intention to create a new organization, the Hindustan National Guards and starting various centres in the form of "Savarkar Canteen" in different parts of Delhi.[89] To give a fillip to this move the Mahasabha shifted its venue of meeting from proposed Ahmedabad to Delhi.[90]

Meetings of the Arya Kumar Sabha, Provincial Hindu Sabha, Hindu Arya Yuvak Sangh and Hindu Students Federation were held on 19th, 20th, 24th and 28th of October respectively in Delhi. In the speeches it was urged that Hindi should be adopted as the state language, the Muslims should now quit the Indian Union, and restrictions on Hindu meetings should be withdrawn. Hindu detenues including L.C. Thatte should be released, the Government of Kashmir should not virtually be handed over to the Muslims, the security demanded from the *Hindu Outlook* and order of suspension against *Sangram* should be cancelled.

During the second half of October, Hindus showed resentment against the imposition of a fine of Rs 10,000 on the people of Paharganj locality, where Dr F.H. Mufti was murdered and by way of protest a hartal was observed.[92] The R.S.S. held the *Vijay Dashmi* Celebration on 23rd October at the Polytechnic College, Kashmiri Gate, Sabzi Mandi, Najafgarh, etc. About 1000 persons gathered at each of the places. Babu Ram of Poona presided over the gathering at the Commercial College Ground. The R.S.S. also held a secret meeting in Delhi Cloth Mill on 22nd October to prevent cow slaughter on the occasion of the Id Festival but nothing untoward happened as the Muslims did not make an attempt to slaughter any cow at all.[93] But the situation became explosive when three Hindu *sadhus* took possession of a Muslim shrine known as *Takiya Daroga* in Faiz Bazar Police Station on 27th October on the plea that it was formerly the temple of Hanuman.[94]

But Muslims were more positive. The Muslim refugees returned in thousands to the city with more confidence than the majority community from Purana Qila,[95] and this was partly the result of the speech delivered by Maulana Abul Kalam Azad, the Education Minister, in the Jama Masjid.[96] He clearly told the audience that the Government of India was not a sectarian government but a national one and was doing its best to protect the interests of the Muslim community. He also added that Jamait-ul-Ulema was the only body to safeguard the interests of the Muslims in India.[97] On the following day the "Dissolve Muslim League Day" was celebrated in the same mosque.[98]

In the second half of November 1947, some excitement had been caused over the alleged prosecution of forty workers of the R.S.S. at Karachi and they had called upon the Government of India to stem the rising tide of insult and injury to Hindus in Pakistan. The membership of R.S.S. was increasing and new sakhas for women were started in Sabzi Mandi, Karol Bagh and Paharganj.[99] The other important event of the fortnight was the criticism of Mahatma Gandhi by Hindus and Sikhs for creating lawlessness and it was resented by the extremist right wing.[100]

In December, the Jamiat-ul-Ulema-i-Hind started a campaign to increase its membership. The nationalist Muslims (about 400) who attended the Indian Muslim Conference at Lucknow welcomed the three-point programme[101] of Maulana Abul Kalam Azad to liquidate communal organizations in India.

Thus, by the end of the year the communal fever started declining. The division of India and Pakistan demoralized the Muslim communal organizations in India. The psychological fear of Muslim community in India, which was not totally irrational, made them defensive. The role of Mahatma Gandhi and the nationalist Muslims were important in this regard. Maulana Abul Kalam Azad made a great contribution in persuading the Muslim community to do away with its communal extremism. But unfortunately it was not the case of Hindu communalism. They were shortsighted and felt victorious as they continued to demand a Hindu nation, with saffron flag and Hinduized culture. It was due to this specificity, communalism did not evanesce with the departure of British imperialism from India. The monster remained alive.

REFERENCES

1. Fortnightly Report for the second half of December 1946, F.No. 1/1947.
2. *Ibid.*
3. *Ibid.*
4. *Ibid.*
5. *Ibid.*
6. *Ibid.*
7. *Ibid.*
8. Fortnightly Report for the first half of January 1947, *ibid.*

9. *Ibid.*
10. Fortnightly Report for the second half of January 1947, *ibid.*
11. Fortnightly Report for the second half of January 1947, *ibid.*
12. Fortnightly Report for the second half of January 1947, *ibid.*
13. *Ibid.*
14. *Ibid.*
15. *Ibid.*
16. *Ibid.*
17. *Ibid.*
18. *Ibid.*
19. Fortnightly Report for the first half of February 1947, *ibid.*
20. *Ibid.*
21. *Ibid.*
22. *Ibid.*
23. *Ibid.*
24. *Ibid.*
25. Fortnightly Report for the second half of February 1947, *ibid.*
26. *Ibid.*
27. *Ibid.*
28. Fortnightly Report for the first half of March 1947, *ibid.*
29. *Ibid.*
30. *Ibid.*
31. *Ibid.*
32. *Ibid.*
33. *Ibid.*
34. *Ibid.*
35. Fortnightly Report for the second half of March 1947, *ibid.*
36. *Ibid.*
37. *Ibid.*
38. *Ibid.*
39. *Ibid.*
40. *Ibid.*
41. *Ibid.*

42. *Ibid.*
43. *Ibid.*
44. *Ibid.*
45. Fortnightly Report for the first half of April, *ibid.*
46. *Ibid.*
47. Published in *The Hindustan Times.*
48. *Ibid.*
49. Madhavacharya to the Chief Commissioner, Delhi, H.F. No.44/47/B, Confidential.
50. *Ibid.*
51. *Ibid.*
52. *Ibid.*
53. Fortnightly Report for the second half of April, *ibid.*
54. *Ibid.*
55. *Ibid.*
56. Fortnightly Report for the first half of April, *ibid.*
57. *Ibid.*
58. *Ibid.*
59. Christie to Banerjee, D.C. No. 674-ST/CC; H.F.No. 51/47, Part B, Confidential.
60. *Ibid.*
61. *Ibid.*
62. Fortnightly Report for the first half of June, *ibid.*
63. *Ibid.*
65. *Ibid.*
66. *Ibid.*
67. *Ibid.*
68. H.F. No. 51/47/B, Confidential.
69. *Ibid.*
70. *Ibid.*
71. *Ibid.*
72. *Ibid.*
73. *Ibid.*
74. *Ibid.*
75. *Ibid.*
76. *Ibid.*
77. *Ibid.*

78. *Ibid.*
79. Fortnightly Report for the first half of July, *ibid.*
80. *Ibid.*
81. Fortnightly Report for the first half of August, *ibid.*
82. Fortnightly Report for the first half of September, *ibid.*
83. *Ibid.*
84. *Ibid.*
85. Fortnightly Report for the first half of October, *ibid.*
86. *Ibid.*
87. *Ibid.*
88. *Ibid.*
89. *Ibid.*
90. *Ibid.*
91. Fortnightly Report for the second half of October, *ibid.*
92. *Ibid.*
93. *Ibid.*
94. *Ibid.*
95. *Ibid.*
96. *Ibid.*
97. *Ibid.*
98. Fortnightly Report for the second half of December, *ibid.*
99. *Ibid.*
100. *Ibid.*
101. *Ibid.*

5

POLICE

Police played a vital role in the 'construction of colonialism' in British India. It was one of the pillars over which the whole superstructure of the mighty British Empire in India rested. It restored law and order, suppressed the rebellious voice of over-exploited Indian masses, provided a defensive shield to the mechanism of colonial draining and created a myth of all powerful British apparatus in the minds of the common Indian folks. It was successful in playing such a crucial role, because it acted as a living organ of British imperialism.

But the gradual Indianization of the British administration in the twentieth century meant also the gradual 'injection of mind' in Indian police. They started thinking, became conscious of their interests, their emotions, their surroundings and the political atmosphere of the country and the world. It became more apparent in the last days of British imperialism and 1947-India saw them in top gear. It means that in a charged atmosphere of Delhi with the communal current, police behaved 'differently', though the changed circumstances also played their role. The changed circumstances can be explained in terms of the so-called transfer of power, the partition of India, the extension of Punjab violence to Delhi, the All-India riots, the influx of the refugees, and their rehabilitation, security arrangements for the refugee camps and to keep them hygienic, and the increased responsibility of the police, etc. It meant that police administrators had also to act as civil administrators along with an added responsibility to provide security and protection to the VIPs. But they lacked the strength in terms of number in a situation of increased responsibility which gave them the excuse to be relaxed. The Indianization of British administration has, however, been overstressed. The British mentality survived. The claim of *'mai-baap'* continued. The backwardness of the country and the uneven development of national consciousness and political awareness still remained a dominant feature and modulated the concept of nationalism. The bureaucracy and the police played a dubious game in the hour of crisis.

It is in this background that the police administration and their role in maintaining peace in Delhi would be examined. Paharganj riot may be a good example to start with. It has already been pointed out that police played a partisan role which is clear from the statistics of the police-after-action where no Muslim was arrested and only Hindus and Sikhs were penalized.[1] Even if their role was evaluated officially by saying that 'the magistrates and police have done excellent job in quelling the recent communal disturbances in the city of Delhi'[2] it would be good to go deep into their mode of operation because any feeling of complacency even after quelling the disturbances would have been disastrous.[3] "We must also not forget that the administration of Delhi has a heavier responsibility, for Delhi is the seat of Government", concluded Randhawa, the D.C.P. in his confidential note.[4] "Anything which happens here has repercussions on the rest of India. Moreover, if work in offices of the government suffers, as it has suffered due to disturbed conditions during the last fortnight, the entire economy of the country will suffer". With this cautious note, Randhawa suggested all the magistrates and police officers of Delhi to discharge their functions with full consciousness of the importance and gravity of the tasks entrusted to them.[5] For this he suggested the following measures:[6]

1. *Curfew:* So long curfew continued, police officers and magistrates should see that it is rigidly imposed. Periodic visits to streets at night time should continue.
2. *Search of Suspects:* Most of the stabbing cases occur between 6-8 A.M. and 5-7 P.M. Some of the assassins go about in tongas and after stabbing their victims jump off or escape in tongas. While patrolling magistrates and police officers should search such suspects in streets for knives and daggers. Already some action has been taken and these had a salutary effect.

During curfew hours, houses of suspected individuals should also be searched. As many people are hiding knives in their houses and have collected piles of bricks, houses of suspected individuals should be searched on a random-sampling principle.

Action on the above lines is particularly necessary in Sadar Bazar police circle. Following figures of casualties during these riots are revealing:

	For the entire city	*For Sadar Bazar*
Dead	28	18
Injured	54	35

Police officers who are concerned with this area should see that no further carnage occurs in this area and *Mirdasi* of Faizganj are properly looked after. Sadar Bazar, Pahari Dhiraj, Bara Hindu Rao and Bahadurgarh Road should receive fullest possible attention.

3. *List of Goondas:* The police officers-in-charge of various police stations should immediately prepare lists of bad characters who commit acts of violence or instigate communal trouble ... complete maps should also be prepared indicating the places where these goondas live, when they are not of shifting type.
4. Intensive action should be taken under the security sections of the Criminal Procedure Code against miscreants and instigators of trouble.
5. *Communal Organizations:* Militant communal organizations like the Rashtriya Swayam Sewak Sangh and the Muslim National Guards should be carefully watched and if any of their members incites trouble, they should be hauled in.
6. *Intensive Patrolling:* Patrolling of streets should continue and places of junctions of Hindu and Muslim mohallas should be carefully watched.
7. *Infiltration of Doubtful Strangers:* During periods of communal tension rumours like "so many Pathans or Rampuriyas have been harboured in a mosque" or "so many Jats are staying in Dharmshalas" have gained currency and caused considerable panic among the people. Infiltration of such doubtful strangers from outside should

be rigorously checked. For this purpose a vigilant watch should be kept on mosques, dharmashalas, orphanages, railway and bus stands and Jumna Bridge.

8. In addition to sentences of rigorous imprisonment, whipping should be given in cases of such dastardly assaults.
9. Hawkers of newspapers, particularly of Urdu and Hindi papers have contributed considerably to existing panic. They should be watched carefully.
10. *Peace Committees:* Such committees should be formed in each mohalla. They should not only promote communal harmony, but should also give specific information to the authorities about bad characters, etc. Their work will be regarded as successful only when the Hindu members give information about Hindu goondas and Muslims, about Muslim goondas.
11. *Broadcasts on Communal Harmony:* Leaders of various communities should be encouraged to broadcast speeches from Delhi Microphone Stations on subjects which are likely to promote communal harmony. Speeches by Hindus on Muslim culture and its contribution to the pan-Indian culture and by Muslims on Hindu culture can be of help in developing mutual esteem. For countering false rumours and for allaying panic, microphone service can be made very useful. Joint celebration of religious festivals also promote good feelings. If Hindus publicly entertain Muslims on their festivals like Dussehra, feelings of fellowship can be promoted.

Here, it looks as if the police became determined to maintain law and order situation in Delhi and it would not permit communal monster to be out of control and an administrative grip would be maintained over anti-social and goonda elements at any cost. But it was only a theoretical position. The police had a peculiar Muslim bias before the month of April as has already been suggested. This particular Muslim bias was countered by the Home Ministry with strong Hindu-and-Sikh bias.[7] The game of communalization of administration was played by two meticulous players. The pressure of Hindu and Sikh interest groups was enormous over the Home Ministry. The Home Ministry under the leadership of Sardar Ballabh Bhai Patel started recognizing itself as representing the interests primarily of the Hindus. It was evident from the questionaire[8] prepared by the Home Ministry regarding the modality of representation of different communities to Delhi police. Its subsequent suggestion[9] to balance the Hindu and Sikh representations in police with those of the Muslim representation was the most significant official move. It was a communal line evident from the simple logic that doing away with communalism would not permit any step to make the institution more communal. The Home member wished that steps should be taken to replace a few Muslim police officers in Delhi by Hindus or Sikhs.[10] The Hon'ble member, Porter reported, "though recognizes that wholesale changes cannot be brought about simultaneously and at once without the risk of dislocating the police administration".[11] He thought, however, that a period of six or eight months should be sufficient period for bringing about the change. Christie was, therefore, directed to take up the matter with the Punjab Government the question of replacing the Muslim officer within the period and as such dates as may be administratively convenient, so that the reduction of Muslim officers to the number necessary to correct the present communal maladjustment be made.[12] The Home member also emphasized that Anglo-Indians in the officer ranks of the police occupied a number of posts in excess of their population ratio and, therefore, object should be achieved as to ensure a representation of Hindus and Sikhs[13] at their place.

The process of balancing of communal representation can be understood by examining the permutations and combinations in police administration in the month for example say March 1947. The strength of the different communities in Delhi police above the rank of inspectors on 1st March 1947 can be shown from the data given below:[14]

S.No.	Rank of the Officer	No. of British	Anglo-Indians	Muslims	Hindus	Sikhs	Total
1.	Supdt. of Police	1	-	-	-	-	1
2.	Add.Supdt. of Police	1	-	-	-	-	1
3.	Dy. Supdt. of Police	-	4	3	1	-	8
4.	Inspectors	-	5	9	2	6	22

During these 30 days, the opportunities which had occurred for re-adjustment of communal proportion on account of-[15]

(i) Death	Nil
(ii) Retirement	Nil
(iii) Reversion to Punjab	One Superintendent of Police and two inspectors had been reverted to Punjab; one Deputy Superintendent of Police was under orders of transfer to Punjab.

Thus Khan Sahib Walli Ullah, a Muslim Deputy Superintendent of Police, was transferred to the Punjab and in his place L. Chuni Lal, a Hindu D.S.P., had come to Delhi.[16] Again the transfer of L.C. Disney to Punjab was also suggested.[17] Again W.D. Robinson was also proceeding on leave with effect from 6 March 1947.[18] The I.G. Police of Punjab, in the mean time was suggested to 'adjust communal representation within next six months'. The communal representation in the Delhi Police after adjustment for the end of the months can be shown from the following statistics.[19]

S.No.	*Rank of the Officer*	*No. of British*	*Anglo-Indian*	*Muslim*	*Hindu*	*Sikh*	*Total*
1.	Supdt. of Police	-	1	-	-	-	1
2.	Add. Supdt.of Police	1	1	1	1	-	4
3.	Dy. Supdt. of Police	-	4	3	2	-	9
4.	Inspectors	-	5	9	2	5	21

The details of the officers of the Delhi Police can be seen in Appendix.[20]

The sanctioned strength of Gazetted Officers and Inspectors in the Delhi Police was:[21]

Senior Superintendent of Police = 1

Superintendent of Police = 4 (including S.P. Enforcement)

Deputy S.P. = 8

Inspectors = 22 (including Inspector in Charge Constituent Assembly)

Of this strength, only 2 posts, viz. Superintendent of Police, Enforcement and Inspector In Charge Constituent Assembly, were arranged from the posts exclusively borne on the Delhi Administration.[22] All the other posts belonged to joint Punjab-Delhi cadre and officers were not brought on deputation.[23] Thus these posts were not a part of deputation reserve of the Punjab Police. If, therefore, it was proposed to replace any of these officers by officers from United Province, there would be a corresponding reduction in the Punjab cadre.

However, in those days of vast expansion and acute shortage of officers, Punjab would find no difficulty whatsoever in absorbing any officer who might be released in this manner. But the danger was that if Punjab felt that their officers were not being appreciated and were being replaced by officers from another province, the Inspector General of Police, Punjab, might move for the reversion of all Punjab officers. This would be somewhat awkward.

It was true that there were no insuperable difficulties for the U.P. officers to master the Punjab Police Rules after due study and experience. But during the period of study and experience they would find it hard and might also find it more difficult than Punjab officers to deal with men and circumstances. However, these were not treated by D.C. Lal, S.S.P. Delhi as insurmountable difficulties and therefore he considered the following posts possibly to be held by officers from U.P. without feeling any undue obstacles due to change of province and conditions:[24]

1. D.S.P., Enforcement - New Officer was yet to arrive, already earmarked for a U.P.Officer.
2. A.S.P. - Present incumbent W.J.H. Fearn. He preferred a Punjab Officer for this post as he has to handle most of the office work and also a fair amount of crime work, office methods, Rules etc.,

were different for different provinces. Similarly Thana working and minor points connected with crime work etc., were different. An officer from U.P. had to take some time to get used of these practices. It may be mentioned here that Fearn had already asked to be sent back to Punjab and after approval of his request and inability of Punjab to replace him, there was possibility to have an officer from U.P.

3. D.S.P./C.I.D. (Security) - Present incumbent A.V.R. Burton. This officer could be from the U.P. because this post did not require any particular provincial method of work, and an officer from the U.P. would be able to pick it up quite easily.
4. One Prosecuting Inspector - Present incumbent Sheikh Ghulam Hussain.
5. One Traffic Inspector - Present incumbent G.F. Gore.
6. Quarter Master Inspector - Present incumbent S. Firdaus Shah.
7. Inspector Protection, C.I.D. - Present incumbent Zeenat Ullah Khan.

For these officers, S.S.P. did not approve of the shift in the light of strong reaction from the Punjab police.[25]

There were nine Anglo-Indian officers[26] of the rank of Inspector and above. One of them, Disney had already been transferred and replaced by S. Tek Singh. Thus only eight officers were left and he dealt with them separately.

1. A.S.P./C.I.D. - He supported the replacement by a Punjab officer.
2. D.S.P./C.I.D. (Security) - This was another post which could be held by an Indian well.

Incidentally, this was also a post which an officer from U.P. could hold.

3. D.S.P., New Delhi - This post meant considerable contact with the Viceregal Lodge and other high officials of New Delhi. Though in the past it was founds that an Anglo-Indian officer was well suited but in the changed circumstances, it could be successfully held by an Indian officer.
4. D.S.P., Lines - Previously an Assistant Superintendent of Police used to be in charge of the lines. During the war, due to shortage of I.P. officers, a D.S.P. was appointed. The D.S.P. posted there was a very efficient police officer and owing to his efficiency, the S.S.P. did not want any change there.
5. Cantonment Inspector - In the past, an Anglo-Indian officer had been found more useful as he had to deal with European personnel and officers. S.S.P. thought it better to continue for a little longer, so long as British troops and British officers continue to remain in the cantonment.
6. Traffic Inspector - Any Indian officer was efficient for the post and might be appointed.
7. Reserve Inspector - It had been customary to have an Anglo-Indian officer as Reserve Inspector in the past as it was found to be in the interest of better discipline. Since the present incumbent Hussain was a good disciplinarian and was well trained in the use of various modern automatic weapons etc., the S.S.P. urged that he should be continued in the post.
8. Inspector Viceregal Guard - This officer was in charge of the Viceroy's Guard and was a personal gunman of the Viceroy. The S.S.P., therefore,

thought it best suited to an Anglo-Indian or a European officer.

On the basis of above recommendation of the S.S.P. the position regarding the Inspector on the 1st July would be[27]

Anglo-Indian	-	4
Muslims	-	8
Hindus	-	5
Sikhs	-	5

In addition, Chaudhari Aminuddin, Deputy Superintendent of Police, Headquarters, had applied for reversion to Punjab and the S.S.P. recommended the application to I.G. Police, Punjab with the request that he be replaced by a non-Muslim officer. At the same time, he had also asked the I.G. Police, Punjab, to revert Inspector Khan Shahib Manzur Wahid to the Punjab and post a non-Muslim officer in his place. In case these recommendations were accepted by the I.G. Police, the position regarding the Deputy Superintendents of Police and Inspectors would be as under:[28]

Deputy Superintendents of Police

Anglo-Indians	-	3
Muslims	-	1
Hindus	-	4

Inspectors

Anglo-Indians	-	4
Muslims	-	7
Hindus	-	6
Sikhs	-	5

Thus, under pressure of Home Ministry the total representations of Hindus and Muslims in Delhi Police for Inspectors and the above police rank was made 15 (4+5+6) as against 8 (1+7) Muslims by 1st July of 1947. This was on all accounts a substantial change.

During June 1947, owing to the current disturbances in Lahore and Amritsar, there appeared dangerous possibilities of violence and rioting in Delhi.[29] All communities were busy making secret war-like preparations. It would be good to go through the precautionary measures the administration adopted.

The following orders under section 144 Cr.P.C. were declared in force:[30]

(a) Orders banning the assembly of five or more persons;

(b) Orders prohibiting processions of ten or more persons, the number of people reduced later to 'five or more';

(c) Orders restricting the manufacture, import, alienation of *lathis* etc.;

(d) Orders prohibiting parades and marches; and

(e) Orders prohibiting the carrying of fire-arms, *lathis*, etc.

Apart from these orders, arrangements had been made with the military authorities for three companies of troops to be standing by in various parts of the urban area from 1st June 1947. Fire engines were also to be distributed as much as possible throughout the urban area and armed guards were to be sent out with them to prevent them from being attacked. Water tanks and rationing godowns were to be specially guarded and special patrols for petrol dumps and fuel dumps had to be arranged. Arrangements were also being made for special testing of telephones and possibly also for additional lines of telephones to be installed for those most concerned with the maintenance of law and order.[31] Orders were being issued for all arms and ammunitions to be deposited by the dealers in the Fort and for compilation of the list of the licensees so that the arms with doubtful persons might be taken care of.[32] Having in view the fact that extremist elements of the society, especially the Sikhs, were using jeeps and command cars to glamorize their communal positions, it was proposed to issue orders prohibiting the use of such vehicles or any vehicle which might look like an armoured car, generally used for military purposes, at least in certain areas, except for official purposes.[33] To deal with the deteriorating condition of Delhi, the police in Delhi demanded an "ordinance" on the line of one proclaimed in the United Provinces whereby police was authorized to shoot at sight in "certain eventualities".[34] In other words, police force in Delhi was trying, at least in theory, to cope with pre-anticipated possibilities of riots.

One important point, we should always have in our mind, is that the police, despite these arrangements, was never sure of its capability to tackle the communal tension, owing to its relatively smaller size. The managers of the police force always tried their best to draw the government's attention towards the problem whenever they found appropriate opportunity.[35] It can best be explained in regard with the question of the recruitment of special police. "As regards the special police, there has been no actual recruitment of special police, nor any such scheme sanctioned", complained Christie.[36] Christie categorically stated to the government that it was virtually impossible to borrow any police from the U.P. Special Armed Constabulary; that the trainees of the Central Administrative Services might be enrolled as special constables; that he should be authorized to recruit a force of about 200 ex-soldiers of all ages, provided they were physically fit, and also ex-V.COs. to form a sort of striking force for an emergency; that this force would have to be sanctioned up to the end of the present financial year.[37] The full strength of constables for Delhi Police was, on paper, only 2779, but the actual was even lesser. Only 2509 was their numerical strength at that time.[38] Even among these relatively small number, about 350 recruits were not properly trained.[39] In other words, the police found itself in 1947 slightly odd with the government's stand. Whether it was deliberate or not was obviously altogether a different question. It is even more difficult to relate this position of the government with the current situation of communal disturbances, since archival sources very scarcely pointed towards such trend. Still, the conjectures and circumstances seek our attention towards this.

A Case Study of Fatehpuri Mosque: The Police Role (24th and 25th July 1947)

In the month of July 1947 the Fatehpuri Mosque became the nerve centre of the *Khaksars,* a group of Muslim fundamentalists comparable to the Hindu Mahasabha or the R.S.S. Using the mosque as a 'refugee centre', the Khaksars tried to transform it as a centre for Islamic propaganda. 'They have been making a nuisance of themselves to the mosque authorities and were also committing illegal acts, i.e., violation of orders under section 144 Cr.P.C., inciting and making inflammable speeches and actions, occasional rallies from the mosques with attacks on police parties, etc." goes on a special official report on Fatehpuri Raid.[40] A complaint under section 448/225 IPC was lodged by the secretary of the Majlis-e-Aukab on 22nd July 1947. Case F.I.R. No. 548 dated 22 July 1947 at about 6 P.M.: two Khaksars armed with *belchas* came out of the Fatehpuri Mosque and started parading on the road in front of the mosque gate.[41] It was, thus, a dangerous situation and needed an organized and well-planned police action to curb the potential source capable of serious disturbance.

A small police party led by Inspector Jaswant Singh, reached the spot and arrested them. The *Khaksars* attacked the police causing sharp-edged injuries to two constables with the edge of their *belchas*.[42] However, they were overpowered. At this, a group of 25 to 30 *Khaksars* armed with *belchas* rushed out of the mosque to rescue them. The Inspector warned them to stay back otherwise he would be compelled to open fire. But they, in very exciting and charged mood, continued to advance and the police was compelled to open fire in "self defence".[43] Three *Khaksars* were hit but they were dragged into the mosque by their comrades. Case FIR No. 554, u/s 148/332/307 was registered in Police Station Kotwali. S.S.P. and D.S.P.(City) immediately reached the Kotwali on receipt of information and necessary precautionary measures were taken.[44] A meeting was then held between the Chief Commissioner, Deputy Commissioner and the Senior Superintendent of Police and it was then decided to raid the Fatehpuri Mosque and 50 to 60 *Khaksars* were arrested. Necessary arrangements were hurriedly organized. The military were called in to stand by in the Fort. In addition to the 54 *Khaksars* arrested in the raid, 24 others were also arrested on the 24th, 12 having been arrested in various places and 12 having been compelled to leave Delhi. Thus the total number of Khaksars arrested on 24lh/25th was 78. Seventy Khaksars were estimated to be in the Mosque and they were expected to leave Delhi peacefully.[45]

Interestingly, the police raided in a very planned manner with minutest possible details at their disposal despite all their shortcomings. They scrutinized and streamlined the raid very efficiently. First, a force was sent under a "Hindu" Inspector, Jaswant Singh who was "forced" to open fire in "self defence" as the official report maintained. All the higher officials with utmost urgency planned the raid and arrested or forced all the *Khaksars* to leave Delhi. With the precise knowledge of their strength at its command shows that some powerful forces were acting from behind. All these positive 'haste' and 'planning' forced one to conclude about changing character of police. From October 1946 to April 1947, police seemed sympathetic towards the Muslim cause, but the changing nature of the national politics and certainty, situation after Independence tilted the balance to the other side. It was not therefore accidental and the Report itself maintains, ".... Although the conduct of the Khaksars was peaceful, while the arrests were being made, yet when they had been put into the prison vans they started shouting slogans. On the last occasion they had contended themselves with "Islam Zindabad", "Khaksar Zindabad", but this time the added "Zulam Hukumat Murdabad", "Nehru Murdabad" and "Patel Murdabad".[46] This transformation in the nature of slogans was sufficient to indicate the involved politics in the raid and arrests.

Collective Fines : Strategy or Politics?

September of 1947 was important so far as the history of police administration in Delhi is concerned. It was 7th September 1947, the long awaited demand to strengthen the police capability in emergency period was granted, though not fully, in form of the extension of Punjab Safety Act, 1947 to the territory of Delhi.[47] According to it:[48]

1.I. Collective fine in a "dangerously" disturbed area may be imposed under section 33 by the 'Provincial Government' or by the District Magistrate on the grounds that the inhabitants of the area have been concerned in the commission of the offences or other actions prejudicial to the maintenance of law and order, etc.

II. An order made by the District Magistrate has to be reported through the Commissioner to the Provincial Government and the Provincial Government "may therefore amend or vary or restrict such order".

III. "A person or a class or section of inhabitants of the area may be exempted from liability to pay the fine".

IV. After imposition of the fine the District Magistrate is to "apportion" the amount among the inhabitants "according to the respective financial means of such inhabitants".

V. The fine is recoverable as a fine or as arrears of land revenue.

VI. Any order passed by the District Magistrate is "subject to revision" by the Commissioner or the Provincial Government.

2. Under section 34 of the Punjab Safety Act, 1947, compensation may be paid to such persons in a dangerously disturbed area (where death or grievous hurt or loss of or damage to property has been caused by or has been ensued from the misconduct of inhabitants of such areas) as have suffered injuries from such misconducts of the inhabitants.
3. "Under the notification of 7.9.1947 extending to the Punjab Public Safety Act, 1947 and the Punjab Disturbed Areas Act of 1947 to Delhi, it has been laid down that all powers of the Provincial Government under these Acts shall be powers of the Central Government as well as the Chief Commissioner of Delhi".
4. Under the notification the whole of the province of Delhi has the similar meaning of section 2 of the Punjab Public Safety Act.
5. So the provisions of sections 33 and 34 of the Punjab Public Safety Act are applicable to Delhi.

Analysis of the Acts extended to Delhi clearly shows that there was a great scope of "political" maneuvering, and political meant in the period of our study "communal". If we go through the provisions of the Act, especially the clauses under quotes here, the adjustment capability of the new provisions became quite clear. This aspect of the Act is, however, difficult to support through official documentation, but one may "sense" it going through the avoidable narratives and correspondence of concerned parties.

It would be good in this context to list the localities where the collective fines were imposed so that disturbances might be checked under the weight of heavy fines. The police authorities classified the disturbed localities under two categories:[49]

(I) Localities with mixed population like Qarol Bagh, Paharganj, and Subzimandi. These places had a mixed population of Hindus, Sikhs and Muslims. Rioting, looting, murder and arson took place on a wide scale in this area (during the year of our study). While in Qarol Bagh, Hindus and Sikhs were the aggressors, in Paharganj and Subzimandi both the major communities were more or less equally matched and were equally to be blamed. In Subzimandi, the Muslims fired automatic weapons from their houses and large numbers of arms and ammunitions were recovered from their houses. It was difficult, the Report[50] goes on, "to apportion blame on any particular community .... Persons who are most to blame are penniless refugees from the West Punjab and Mill hands". From a population of this nature not much could be recovered. A collective fine, the Report hoped, could act as a deterrent if it is speedily collected.

(II) The second category was consisted of the Muhallas exclusively Muslim dominated areas. They were termed as localities liable for collective fines on account of their participation in firing over police and military. They were:

(a) Turkman Gate Area P.S. Faiz Bazar

(b) Chhata Lal Mian P.S. Faiz Bazar

(c) Gali Shah Tara P.S. Hauz Kazi

(d) Gali Sher Afgan Bahadur Ballimaran Mohalla P.S. Hauz Kazi

(e) Phatak Habash Khan P.S. Kotwali

(f) Kisan Ganj, Hathi Khana P.S. Sadar Bazar

(g) Chamrewalan Bazar P.S. Sadar Bazar

The categorization of the Muhallas clearly shows that the determination of the localities were clearly tilted in favour of one community. It is interesting to note that the predominantly Hindu or Sikh dominated areas found no place in the categorization of the localities, as if these two communities had nothing to do with the disturbances. Only one village, dominated by Hindu Jati, were named, and that this village Barwala too possessed a substantial Muslim population. Two more arguments[51] were developed, which was used to "soften" the burden of penalties, i.e. (a) the aggrieved parties' inability to pay the taxes and (b) the inability of the police and magisterial staffs to collect it on account of their insufficient number required for the implementation of the collective fines. These two limitations were used differentially depending upon political permutations and combinations. Thus, the strategy, adopted against the communal disturbances, transformed itself into "politics of communalism". The Chief Commissioner of Delhi, Shahibzada Khurshid, therefore, reasoned,[52] "I was, therefore, unaware of the circumstances which led the Government to decide that imposition of collective fines at this stage was not desirable or necessary". It shows that the collective fines were imposed or suspended by "political circumstances".

Government, Police and Lahiry Case

In an order[53] dated 4 September 1947 which was passed under section 3 of the Punjab Criminal Law Shahibzada Khurshid, the Chief Commissioner of Delhi, required, Asutosh Lahiry, General Secretary of the Hindu Mahasabha residing at that time in the Hindu Mahasabha Bhavan, New Delhi, to leave the territory of Delhi within "24 hours of the receipt of the order". The main suspicion against Asutosh Lahiry was that he had been training Hindus and Sikhs in the manufacture of explosives and bombs and an "inflammatory" leaflet attributed to Lahiry in that period of time when the partition of Punjab and the consequent movement of refugees with tales of the atrocities committed to them made it very sensitive.[54] By any standard used for evaluation, such decision of the administration seems very legitimate and that too in the light of Lahiry's frank approval.[55] "... and I need not hesitate to say that I took a leading part in organizing their defence of the Hindus there in Calcutta, during the darkest days of communal frenzy, as he himself would like to say."

Now the government with the convenience of the Home Minister, Vallabh Bhai Patel, adopted a very strange position.[56] In his view, this order was "politically" inexpedient and suggested the concerned official to distinguish such potentially dangerous elements into two categories[57] prominent persons like Asutosh Lahiry and the general populace. The police administration was advised to take action at its will in the latter case but they had to take prior permission of the government if they were to take action against the prominent person like Lahiry.[58] Government came out with another interesting excuse:[59]

> Incidentally Asutosh Lahiry resides permanently in Calcutta and it is understood that he has been here this time since about the first week of August. The 'casual' source reports of the C.I.D. mention several other names as being responsible for organizing subversive activities on the part of

> Hindus and Sikhs. It is not clear why no action has been taken against any of these persons. These persons presumably belong to the more permanent elements of the Delhi population and government finds it rather difficult to follow that Mr. Lahiry who has been only a casual visitor to Delhi should be considered to be so particularly dangerous. It was, on these grounds that the serving of the externment order on Lahiry was characterized as the "most inopportune and inexpedient".[60]

It was, therefore, suggested that the order of externment passed against Lahiry should be "cancelled immediately",[61] and it was cancelled subsequently.

The Lahiry case, one can clearly visualize, was a clear pointer of a "nexus in making" between the Congress at centre, the Hindu Mahasabha and the Delhi Police Administration.

REFERENCES

1. Home File Mo. 113/46, Part C, Confidential.
2. *Ibid.*
3. *Ibid.*
4. *Ibid.*
5. *Ibid.*
6. *Ibid.*
7. Home File No. 27/1947, Part B, Confidential.
8. *Ibid.*
9. *Ibid.*
10. Christie to Robinson, *ibid.*
11. Porter to Christie, *ibid.*
12. *Ibid.*
13. *Ibid.*
14. Home File No. 27/47, Part B, Confidential.
15. *Ibid.*

16. *Ibid.*
17. *Ibid.*
18. *Ibid.*
19. *Ibid.*
20. Appendix.
21. *Ibid.*
22. *Ibid.*
23. *Ibid.*
24. *Ibid.*
25. *Ibid.*
26. *Ibid.*
27. Christie to Banerjee, *ibid.*
28. *Ibid.*
29. Home File No. 51/47, Part B, Confidential.
30. *Ibid.*
31. *Ibid.*
32. *Ibid.*
33. *Ibid.*
34. *Ibid.*
35. *Ibid.*
36. *Ibid.*
37. *Ibid.*
38. *Ibid.*
39. *Ibid.*
40. Home File No.57/47-C, Part B, Confidential
41. *Ibid.*
42. *Ibid.* *
43. *Ibid.*
44. *Ibid.*
45. *Ibid.*
46. As S.S.P. reported, *ibid.*
47. Home File No. 73/47, Part B, Confidential.
48. *Ibid.*
49. *Ibid.*
50. *Ibid.*
51. *Ibid.*
52. *Ibid.*

53. Home File No. 66/47, Part C, Confidential.
54. *Ibid.*
55. Lahiry to Khurshid, dated 19 September 1947, *ibid.*
56. *Ibid.*
57. *Ibid.*
58. *Ibid.*
59. *Ibid.*
60. *Ibid.*
61. *Ibid.*

6

CONCLUSION: COMMUNALISM AND COMMUNAL RIOTS

The ultimate expression of communalism has been the 'riots'. For an average intellectual, communalism and communal riots are synonymous. The scholars of history, on the other hand, distinguish very clearly both the categories. Communalism, for them, has been a long-term evolutionary process (especially in the context of the period under study) which at first assumed an ideological formulation; the ideological formulation created the social class, necessary for its 'reproduction'; the social class, in its turn, found its expression in the contemporary political behaviour; the so evolved political behaviour culminated in the form of political organizations; these political organizations became the radiating centres that continuously radiated the 'signs' and 'symbols'; these 'signs' and 'symbols' on their part helped the creation of 'social cleavages'; the social cleavages meant assertions of communal interests and politics which finally culminated into riots, bloodshed and social fragmentations. From Bipan Chandra to Gyanendra Pandey, from Sociologists to the economic reductionists, from Imperialist School to the Marxist School, all of them have tried to explain communalism and communal riots in more or less similar theoretical formulation, already-explained above.

Though it is not a proper place to go deep into the assertion that David Page, Sumit Sarkar, Gyanendra Pandey and Bipan Chandra belong to the same intellectual class with cosmetic differences, it should still be stated that communalism as an 'ideology', a 'contested ideology', an 'imagined ideology', an 'economic expression', a 'scramble for available sources', a product of 'divide and rule' policy, a 'scramble of available opportunities' and so on and so forth, all are parts of a universal 'game-plan', stated above. None of the theories are contradictory to others; all of them supplement one another, whether one says it 'ideology', or 'structure' or 'construction' or any other imported/imagined terminology. With this understanding in mind no attempt has been made here to evolve another variant of this technology.

One more point which needs to be stressed while discussing "communal riots" is that communal riots involve varying degrees of violence. The 'communal violence' is, however, altogether a different category than 'criminal violence', 'social violence', and the 'Violent Revolution' of the Marxist philosophy. 'Violence' adopted by criminals is generally on localized scale without any class or community affiliation; but 'Social Violence' or the Marxist' 'Violent Revolution' always identifies itself with the category of 'class'. The only difference between 'Social Violence' and the violence of 'Marxist Revolution' is of the degree while the Marxist Revolutions are bloody and happen on a very large scale, the 'social violence' is in the nature of 'everyday forms of resistance' between different classes. The 'communal riots', on the other hand, are generally the result of the mobilization at "community level" on "religious issues" in which economics often plays an important role. This distinction of the categories of violence should always be in the mind while studying the communal riots.

As far as the pattern of communal riots in Delhi in 1947 is concerned, two waves of the 'riots' can easily be observed. The first wave lasted slightly longer, i.e., from March to May, covering a span of three months. The second wave, generally termed as September riots, obviously precipitated in the month of September. Despite these two waves, the sporadic occurrence of the riots of relatively lesser magnitude can be witnessed almost throughout the year. In this sense, the year 1947 for Delhi was the year of 'communal riots'. This pattern creates problems from analytical point of view. In a changed atmosphere throughout the period under study, the fluctuation of the communal consciousness over time is bound to be difficult to measure. Another important limitation in this case is the determination of the extent of the role played by the economic rivalry in the making of the riots. Once the mind of the communities was charged with 'communal emotions', the economic considerations played the deciding role.

[A] The First Wave

The immediate causes of the First Wave of communal riots starting from the month of March 1947 were the events in Punjab and the meeting of the working committee of the Muslim League at Karachi.[1] The Punjab Government's decision to ban the R.S.S. and the Muslim National Guards came as a sudden surprise and caused much excitement which was increased by the arrest of many of the Muslim League leaders.[2]

The other surprise came in the form of sudden withdrawal of the ban. The tension, however, remained as the working committee of the Muslim League decided not to join the Constituent Assembly and demanded its dissolution which charged the politics of Punjab. The magnetic effect of this politically charged atmosphere soon started electrifying the political climate of Delhi. The Punjab development provided the needed hydration for the decaying Muslim League due to their internal dissentions, facing the danger of becoming moribund.[3] 'The young extremist elements with communist sympathies who had come to the fore as a result of the resignation of their rivals', the official report maintained, 'have strengthened their position with their campaigns, public meetings, hartals and processions'.[4] This agitation gave a fillip to the Delhi Muslim National Guards.

These developments in Punjab, along with the strengthening of the right wing within the Muslim community, activated the Hindu militants to politicize the ban on the R.S.S. in Punjab. The R.S.S. decided to arrange a strong rally of the Hindu militants on the communal issues.[5] The ban became the symbol of the 'molestation' of the Hindu mind, the Hindu militants claimed, and Hindu identity. The officials were also called communalization as radicalism. The 'extreme radicalism' of the Muslim paper *Dawn* provided the required 'political capital'[6] to the leaders of the Hindu community to ignite the imagination of the masses.

The protest of the butchers jointly with the Jamiat-ul-Quresh, the agitation against the new Rent Control Bill for the territory of Delhi by Anjuman-I-Millat and a protest against not allowing elephants in the procession of Id-ul-Milad, made the 'balance of communal sensitiveness' unstable.[7] In a working committee meeting of the Hindu Mahasabha, a resolution was passed which warned the country that "the Muslim League is preparing a direct action".[8] It called on "all sections of the people to mobilize under their resources, to meet this threat and to maintain the peace of the country" and also recommended that "the Constituent Assembly should proceed with its work as a fully sovereign body to draw up a constitution for Akhand Hindu India with a strong Central Government".[9] It also emphasized the necessity for co-operating with other Hindu volunteer organizations such as the R.S.S. so that "their help may be made available in times of need".[10] The process of political polarization was thus going on with a great pace.

Towards the end of February, the distinction between political and communal got blurred, as experienced by Christie, the Chief Commissioner.[11] The above stated trend along with serious disturbances in Punjab, culminating into the resignation the Unionist Ministry, communalized the politics of Delhi taking into its grasp almost all the social classes. The scarcity of the news contained in the official communiques issued by the Punjab authorities helped in the spread of "wild rumours" and the publication of "what are probably garbled and exaggerated reports" did worsen the situation already deteriorating.[12] The leaders of the Muslim National Guards and Bazm-i-Pakistan started rumouring the strategy of "defensive precautions for the protection of Muslim community" which created "suspicions" and "counter-suspicions". Under the speedy flow of the communal 'signs' and 'symbols' the nationalist Muslims were goaded to criticize publicly Master Tara Singh for his provocative and inflammable speeches, which they thought were the reason of the rioting by Hindu-Sikh combine.[13] Once again, the official report made no distinction between real and unreal. It gave a good chit to the Master and dismissed the utterances of nationalist Muslims as communal.

The activities of the Muslim organizations resulted in 'negative' reaction among Hindus and Sikhs. The R.S.S., the Hindu Mahasabha and the Akal Regiment along with many other communal forces reacted strongly to the impending partition, Muslim actions and a threat of Muslim state. Following the line, the Hindu and Sikh communalists of Delhi planned jointly to celebrate the Anti-Pakistan Day.[14] An Anti-Pakistan Council of Action was formed in Delhi, members of which were primarily "young and irresponsible" elements of the Hindu and Sikh communities including the always volatile students.[15] Hindu and Sikh shopkeepers supported them by closing their shops and the industrial workers preferred to remain absent in their respective factories.[16] In the military cantonment, about 2000 Hindu and Sikh workers of the military depots organized a strike in their support and the residents of Lodi Colony held an "Anti-Pakistan meeting" in the evening.[17]

Two more happenings in the mean time helped to deteriorate communal stability. First, the resolution passed by the Congress Working Committee recommending the partition of both Bengal and Punjab as a solution of the communal problem of these provinces, were not liked by the Muslims who realized that its acceptance would merely reduce their Pakistan

consciousness and this consciousness became the driving force which deepened the 'tension', and suspicion to a more critical point. Another point, which needs our attention is that it was not 'imagined community' that produced the communal divide, but it was 'mismanagement of community consciousness' that became the inevitable factor.

Police, Government and 'Insecure Individuals': A Case Study of Connaught Place Area

A complaint was made by one Sayed Himmat Ali of Connaught Place of New Delhi according to which two 'Sikh gentlemen' enquired about the Muslim citizens of the area. In communally charged circumstances, the meaning of such enquires were obvious. There was an instance in which some houses of the non-Muslim residents of Connaught Place were marked by someone at night.[37] To have a clear grasp of the problem it would be good to go through the complaint itself:[38]

(a) "... the fact of two Sikh gentlemen going to their shops and making detailed enquiries as to the correct location of their houses, resided by the members of the Muslim community, number of inmates of the houses, the occupation and service and whether they slept inside or outside, which they had no business to do".

(b) That this was not a single example of such activities and that "other houses too have been visited similarly for enquiries, on some pretext or the other".

(c) The coincidal incident, above referred to, clearly points out to one thing, viz. a deliberate, well-organized and systematic plan on the part of the members of the Sikh community to reconnoiter and pick out the Muslim houses and to attack them when they find for them a convenient opportunity to do so".

(d) There was also a rumour afloat that the Sikhs who had been assembled in a very large number in the *Gurudwaras* in New Delhi were planning a big attack on isolated Muslim houses on 30th October.

The police was to provide them the needed security and to ensure that proper action was to be taken "promptly and immediately". What the police actually did is clear from D.C. Lal's (S.S.P.) letter to Randhava[39] which goes on as "Enquiries into the incidents mentioned above have been made. So far no trace of the suspects can be had. There are a number of Sikh refugees in Delhi who have come from Punjab. They move about in the usual course of the day. It has not been possible to trace any special significance to the Sikh youths..." Government's resolve and determination of the police resulted in little success even when places of shelter for the Sikh refugees were limited. A rational view forced one to conclude that police under the leadership of the Home Ministry decided to remain 'inactive'.

On 23rd April, there was again a resurgence of communal trouble. Five incidents took place in Sadar Bazar, a Muslim was found dead in Talkatora Gardens, New Delhi; a Muslim was stabbed on the top of the Ridge in Civil Lines, etc.[40] The total number of casualties since the trouble began on 23 March 1947 were as follows:[41]

	Muslims	Hindus	Sikhs	Total
Killed	15	6	1	22
Injured	28	35	4	67

None of these casualties had been caused by police or military action.

Our conclusion that the 'disturbances' were more 'costly' to the Muslims than the Hindus and Sikhs, even if taken jointly, is clear from that till 23 April, the number of Muslims killed were 15, while only 6+1=7 were killed from both, the Hindu and Sikh communities, less than half of the number of the Muslims.

The casualties on 23rd and 24th April:[42]

	Muslims	Hindus	Sikhs	Total
Killed	5	2	1	8
Injured	4	8	-	12

The trend was almost similar.

The casualties on 26th, 27th and 28th April:

	Muslims	Hindus	Sikhs	Total
Killed	5	-	-	5
Injured	28	37	5	70

The trend, thus, can be confirmed from the data available.

Communal Riots in Rural Delhi: A Case Study of Gurgaon

On the morning of 17th March, certain Hindus of Rewari put into circulation a story that a Muslim had stabbed a Hindu boy.[44] 'Stabbing has a reason, one cannot deny, but it certainly was not communal', argues the Report. As soon as the Hindus had given this story circulation there arose a panic in and around Rewari. The Superintendent of Police along with Additional District Magistrate "very wisely" monitored the situation. Still, three unpleasant incidents[45] were recorded:

1. Certain Hindu villagers tried unsuccessfully to stop a train.
2. Two Muslims were temporarily detained as 'hostages' in a Hindu village; and
3. A party of Muslims returning from Jahazgari cattle fair in Rohtak District were attacked and mildly beaten by Hindu villagers about six miles north of Rewari.

These incidents were the 'signals' of the possible communal 'bloodbath' on 23rd March, and thereafter, after the celebration of the *Pakistan Day.*

On 23rd March, there was a severe disturbance at Hodal which was at the opposite end of the district from Rewari. Ten Muslims were killed in this riot and nearly 30 Muslims were seriously injured. Twenty to thirty private houses ad many shops owned by the Muslims were burnt.[47] In the official sources, this incident was characterized as clearly 'unexpected' without "any substantial reason" - "Not even the Muslims of Hodal itself had been anticipating the trouble".[48]

Yet, the official report itself hinted a Congress-Police combine, though the report regarded it "a story", not the fact.[49] A member of the Congress Working Committee and a Hindu Head Constable of the security police had been going round Hodal in a jeep during the disturbance encouraging the Hindu rioters.... Mehta, a member of the Congress Working Committee, was at Seth Kaikhusro's factory in which he held a share when the disturbance started. After some time, he and the Seth came in their jeep to the police post. There they met Qazi Mumtaz Hussain, Secretary of the District Muslim League and a resident of Hodal and certain other notables. They then set out for Palwal in the jeep to obtain assistance. About half way there they met Sub-Divisional Officer coming towards Hodal in his car with Tahsildar. On being told that a disturbance was in progress at Hodal, S.D.O. went back to Palwal with Tahsildar to obtain police reinforcements and Mehta took the jeep back to Hodal. After putting down some of the passengers he made two or three rounds of the town in his jeep. He was accompanied by a Hindu Head Constable of the Security police and that this Head Constable was armed with a shot gun which he had obtained from a Hindu licensee. Mehta will no doubt say that after having informed the authorities of the troubles he then made every effort to control the town until the police could arrive with S.D.O. Both Mehta and the head constable knew Hodal well. Both must have recognized many of the rioters. If these two men had been acting in real good faith they would have given the names of the rioters, whom they saw. Neither had done so. It would then appear that Mehta first won himself as a Congress leader by giving information of the trouble to the authorities and then proved as the leader of his own community by warning the rioters to make themselves scarce before the police could arrive to arrest them.

Among indirect causes of the Hodal disturbance should be included the activities of Pt. Jiwan Lal, M.L.A.

and the Jat panchayats which was held at Bharatpur in the middle of March.[50] There was no doubt that Pt. Jiwan Lal, Mehta and other Congress leaders had been devoting particular attention to Hodal and its neighbourhood. There was also no doubt that the Jat panchayats which was attended by S. Baldev Singh and Ch. Lehri Singh in addition to local Jat notables attracted particular attention in the neighbourhood of Hodal which is the nearest point in this district to Bharatpur.

On the day before the disturbance at Hodal, the S.D.O. conducted the elections of president and vice presidents of the Hodal municipal committee. One of those contesting was Qazi Mumtaz Hussain, Secretary of the District Muslim League. He was elected Junior Vice-President. This man became very unpopular in recent months among an element of the Hindu population at Hodal. S.D.O. too had been extremely critical of his activities. But he was no worse than the many black marketing Hindu merchants of the town whom S.D.O. had not been criticizing. The elections of President and vice-presidents on the day before the disturbance night well have aggravated communal tension in the town. It is certainly noteworthy that well over half the victims of the riot were residents of the ward in the town from which Qazi Mumtaz Hussain had been elected and were his supporters.[51]

23rd March was a particularly.suitable day for the Hindus of Hodal to make an attack on the Muslims. As it was Sunday the shops of the leading merchants were closed and therefore could not easily be looted. As the shops were closed, the usual crowd of villagers from the country was not in the town. Moreover as the Muslim Assistant Sub-Inspector of Police had taken advantage of some rather flimsy excuse to be absent from the town in order to arrange his own marriage,[52] there was nobody present to exercise effective control. "If the S.D.O. had made any enquiries on the previous day from the local police he would have found that the A.S.I., was not present and might have saved the riot by insisting that adequate police arrangements be made", claimed the Report.

Hence he was in the town on the day before the riot and S.D.O. undoubtedly met local notables. He seems to have been so little worried about the state of the town that he did not even bother to enquire whether the local police was able to control anything which might occur. Palwal followed Hodal shortly after the disturbance had started.[53] Having met Mehta on the way he might have gone straight to Hodal in Mehta's jeep and sent Tehsildar back to Palwal for police reinforcements. His mere arrival would probably have ended the riot. Instead he wasted a full hour by going back to Palwal with Tehsildar.

In the northern Mewat the trouble started when some Meos stole a buffalo from a Hindu Ahir village.[54] As they were taking the buffalo away a party of Meos attacked them. They did not inflict any serious injury. Even so the Ahirs took the matter seriously and the Ahirs and other Hindu villagers assembled in large numbers near Hassanpur Taoru on 29th March. S.P. and a platoon of Gorkhas arrived in time to prevent this crowd from doing any mischief. They arrested about 75 people and dispersed the rest.

This incident had taken place right on the border of Mewat, an eighty per cent Muslim area, and of the eighty per cent Hindu area beyond. A clearly defined boundary between these two areas runs through this district from the United Provinces border just to the west of Hodal up to Bhundsi, then west for a few miles and finally south to the Alwar border. Hassanpur Taoru is close to the northern tip of Mewat. The subsequent heavy disturbances were confined to the sector of Mewat border between Bhundsi and Alwar border.

An attempt was made the day after the incident at Hassanpur Taoru to hold panchayats. Unfortunately the attempt failed and in the afternoon the Meos burned the Gujar village of Kota Khandeola.[55] Next day the Hindus retaliated by burning four Meo villages - Sakatpur and Ghairatpurbas in the morning and Dahri and Gangani later in the day. On 1st April the Meos retaliated by burning Badgujar, Bisar Akbarpur, Khirki and Baghanki. Up to this point all the villages had been evacuated before being burnt and casualties were extremely light. Next morning the Hindus started trouble someway to the south and attacked from the neighbourhood of Dharuhera burning three Meo villages - Ghatal Khurd in Alwar State and Khori Kalan presumably assuming that the Hindus would not attack through state territory had not evacuated their village. Twenty-six were killed including many women and children.[56] This episode thoroughly roused the Meos who burned Rathiwas, Akera and Ghatal Kalan that evening and next morning Nainwal, Sabrawas, Pachgaon and Bhudka together with the adjoining hamlet of Dona Khari. They also burned what had been left in certain other villages which they had attacked earlier. Meanwhile the Hindus retaliated by burning the Meo village of Untaon. In giving this list of villages burnt I have omitted mention of villages in which only a few huts or a few heaps of grain were burnt.

The disturbances had started in most inaccessible part of the district. Many of the villages attacked were surrounded by rocky hills, sand hills and ravines. It was quite impossible for ordinary trucks to move about in this sort of country. Fully equipped police and infantry could not hope to cover more than three miles an hour. On the other hand lightly dressed villagers could cover anything up to five miles an hour. In these circumstances it proved almost impossible at first to do anything effective against the large gangs of both communities which were roaming the country side.[57] After the Khori Kalan episode the Meos threw over all caution and started streaming across the main road between Taoru and Rewari. This gave the police and military forces and the Alwar forces a chance of opening fire. Furthermore on the morning of 3rd April, a Gorkha officer proved the value of a jeep by chasing a crowd of Meos as it was leaving a burning village and/by opening fire from his jeep. At the same time a considerable amount of loot was recovered on 3rd morning. Anything up to 200 rounds were fired in this district by the police and by the military forces. Though full figures of the victims were not available but understandably that about 20 persons were killed - all Muslims.[58]

After the firing on 2nd evening and 3rd morning there was no further trouble in the Taoru neighbourhood of this district. There was however a further outbreak of trouble just over the Alwar border during the early hours of 5th April. A Hindu crowd almost certainly starting from Andrampur Bas in this district set fire to Kalaks, Shahpur and Singpur - three Meo villages in Alwar State - and at the same time the Meos burnt the Hindu village of Balbirpur. Since then there has been no further attempt by a large crowd to set any village on fire. If the total of villages of each community burnt, both in this district and in Alwar State, is taken, it will be found that each community did about as much damage as it received. The Meos however suffered heavier casualties than the Hindus in the disturbances on account of police and army firing.

Throughout this period Rewari tahsil had been most unsettled. Two serious incidents were reported. Four Muslims who were driving goats were attacked near Khalilpur Railway Station by some Hindus, probably from the mob which the S.P. had dispersed at Hassanpur Taoru on 29th March. Three were killed and one got away to report the matter. Some Muslims were also attacked and injured by Hindus on their way to Shahjahanpur in the southern part of Rewari tahsil where they were going to draw their pensions.

There were also several fires, some of them serious, in the towns of the district. At Rewari there was a fire in which over a hundred houses occupied by Hindu Gujars were burnt. In Sohna there were two little fires and later a big fire in which over a hundred houses were burnt, mostly occupied by *chamars, malis* and *qasais*. In Gurgaon a pile of fodder in the *gowshala* was burnt one night and some days later 6 to 7 houses occupied by Muslims were burnt. There was a report of two small fires in Nuh town. Though accidental fires can easily occur at this time of the year, it is inconceivable that all these fires were accidental. The Delhi Cantonment Ordnance Depot Fire Brigade rendered great help in dealing with some of these fires.

On the night between the 2nd and 3rd April

Gurgaon town itself was in a high state of panic. The Commissioner himself did much to restore confidence. Next day the town was practically deserted. Even lawyers did not stay in the *Kutchery* compound in the hope that clients might appear. Since the disturbances in the Taoru neighbourhood have been brought under control, the public in Gurgaon itself has slowly regained confidence.

In all about 20 villages in this district and 5 in Alwar State have been burnt. Large quantities of grain both stored in houses and piled in the threshing floor had been destroyed. Considerable damage to house property had been done in Hodal, Rewari and Sohna. The number of killed however in all these disturbances, in the other connected incidents and as a result of police and military firing cannot be more than one hundred. There had of course been further casualties in Alwar State.[59]

The Second Wave

The most outstanding event of India in the 20th century was the Independence of the Indian State. Evaluating the month of August from any standard, its importance cannot be undermined. Culmination of many trends and processes, that started from the 'Great Revolt of 1857' and the 'Foundation of the Congress', the so-called 'Transfer of Power' became the part of "nostalgia" for an average Indian, rich or poor, of any class or community. But, below the surface of this 'pure' and 'sacred' current lay the dirty, polluted, bloody, communal 'ditches' which undermined the importance and glory of the former.

The historical occasion was celebrated in a befitting

manner and the enthusiasm was genuine and universal. The celebration was not marred by any untoward incident. There was no hostile demonstration by either the *Khaksars* or the Hindu Mahasabha. Police arrangements were excellent bearing in mind that the Independence Day Celebration coincided with Jamiat-ul-Wida. But the award of the Punjab Boundary Commission caused dissatisfaction amongst the Sikh community, who were particularly apprehensive about the fate of their co-religionists in the canal colonies which was to be included in Pakistan.[60] The Hindu Mahasabha, on 9th and 10th August called the All India Hindu convention. Held in New Delhi with V.D. Savarkar as the President, passed a resolution demanding that the National Flag of India should be "the saffron coloured Hindu Flag", that Hindi should be made the *lingua franca* of the country, that a new Constituent Assembly should be elected and that Pakistan should be made part of Hindustan.[61] Seth Ram Krishna Dalmiya along with Maharaja of Bharatpur and Sibban Lal Saxena and many others while presiding over the cow protection conference strongly criticized Jinnah for not paying any heed to the miserable plight of Muslim refugees from the Indian States. In other words, very strong elements of communal disharmony existed in parallel to the process of the 'Transfer of Power'.

In this sphere of mutual suspicion, tension and sporadic violence, a new variable came on the surface in the form of influx of refugees from West Punjab which finally burst into an "orgy of murder, loot and arson" in the first week of September.[63] Disturbances were not confined to the city alone but also spread to the rural areas. In fact the trouble started from the latter and then swept over the city.[64] A large number of Hindus attacked the village Barwala causing more than 300 deaths.[65] The magnitude of the figure of death clearly shows that the intensity of the riot was at the highest point during the disturbances, when one is comparing it with any of the riots in pre-Independence India. Places of worship were burnt and property looted. The remaining Muslims in the rural areas were collected at villages Punjab Khor, Chhatarpur and Tihar and were provided with military and police protection. Village Punjab Khor was also attacked by a mob of about 25,000, but with the timely arrival of the military the situation was saved and Muslims were safely evacuated to Bahadargarh.[66] However, the mobilization of about 25,000 people for violence was tremendous and it fully explains the very high level of communal hatred.

In Delhi city, Qarol Bagh, Subzimandi and Paharganj were scenes of bitter communal fight.[67] Hindus and Sikhs were definitely the aggressors in Qarol Bagh area.[68] In Subzimandi, Muslims who were better armed and had a lot of illicit arms in their possession, caused a good deal of damage by firing with machine guns and sten guns from their houses.[69] In the Turkman Gate area also, the damage was caused with a sten gun.[70]

In the second half of September, the communal situation improved, thanks to "the firm action taken by the military and better patrolling organized by the police".[71] But this did not end the apprehensions of the Muslims as the sporadic assaults continued in few localities. Special Muslim Magistrates and special police officers were appointed in consultation with the leaders of the Jamiat-ul-Ulema and nationalist Muslims to win the confidence of the Muslims.[72] The most decisive factor however, appeared in the form of Mahatma Gandhi's arrival in Delhi and his visits to Muslim Mohallas helped considerably in restoring the morale of the Muslims.[73]

Analysis of these two great waves clarifies, thus, the 'anatomy' and 'physiology' of the communal riots. An attempt has been made to locate the 'role of rumour', 'the continuous process of imagined community', 'the contested identities', along with many 'recent' variables of communalism. Traces or rather seeds of such 'giant' concepts can be traced, if one is equipped with 'microscopic vision', otherwise attempts made are bound to be abortive. The best thing, therefore, is to move towards more 'crude' and 'natural concepts' with strong affinity to the 'historical realities' which is divorced of the 'abstract' philosophies and a 'very heavy' inter-disciplinary approach. The 'anatomy' and 'physiology' of the communal riots as far as Delhi in 1947 is concerned, revolves round interaction and mutual interplay of the three concepts, namely, 'suspicion', 'tension' and 'communal violence'.

REFERENCES

1. Fortnightly Report of the second half of January 1947, F.No. 1/1947, B Confidential.
2. *Ibid.*
3. *Ibid.*
4. *Ibid.*
5. *Ibid.*
6. *Ibid.*
7. Fortnightly Report for the first half of February, F.No. 1/1947.C, Part B, Confidential.
8. *Ibid.*
9. *Ibid.*
10. *Ibid.*

11. Fortnightly Report for the first half of March, F.No. 1/ 1947, C, Part B, Confidential.
12. *Ibid.*
13. *Ibid.*
14. *Ibid.*
15. *Ibid.*
16. *Ibid.*
17. *Ibid.*
18. *Ibid.*
19. *Ibid.*
20. Fortnightly Report for the second half of March.
21. F.No. 36/47-C, Part B, Confidential.
22. *Ibid.*
23. *Ibid.*
24. *Ibid.*
25. *Ibid.*
26. *Ibid.*
27. *Ibid.*
28. *Ibid.*
29. *Ibid.*
30. *Ibid.*
31. *Ibid.*
32. *Ibid.*
33. *Ibid.* [Report on 29th March].
34. *Ibid.*
35. *Ibid.*
36. *Ibid.*
37. *Ibid.*
38. *Ibid.*
39. *Ibid.*
40. *Ibid.*
41. *Ibid.*
42. *Ibid.*
43. *Ibid.*
44. Confidential Fortnightly Report of Gurgaon District, 10.4.47, F.No. 38/47B.
45. *Ibid.*

46. *Ibid.*
47. *Ibid.*
48. *Ibid.*
49. *Ibid.*
50. *Ibid.*
51. *Ibid.*
52. *Ibid.*
53. *Ibid.*
54. *Ibid.*
55. *Ibid.*
56. *Ibid.*
57. *Ibid.*
58. *Ibid.*
59. *Ibid.*
60. Fortnightly Report for the first half of August, F.No. 1/ 1947B, confidential.
61. *Ibid.*
62. *Ibid.*
63. *Ibid.*
64. *Ibid.*
65. *Ibid*
66. *Ibid.*
67. *Ibid.*
68. *Ibid.*
69. *Ibid.*
70. *Ibid.*
71. *Ibid.*
72. *Ibid.*
73. *Ibid.*

APPENDIX I

STATEMENT SHOWING THE NAME OF THE DELHI POLICE OFFICERS STATIONED IN OLD DELHI, THE NOTIFIED AREAS AND NEW DELHI OF AND ABOVE THE RANK OF INSPECTOR

OLD DELHI

Name

1. Sh. D.C. Lal
2. Mr. F.H.G. Bridgman, I.P.
3. Sh. Malik. Ata Mohd Noon
4. Sh. I.L. Malhotra
5. Mr. A.V.R. Burton
6. Sh. Jagan Nath.
7. Sh. Mirza Abdul Saeed.
8. Sh. Mohd Amin-ud-Din
9. Sh. Gulam Hussain.
10. Sh. K.S. Manzur Wahid.
11. Sh. S. Dial Singh

12. Sh. Wazir Ali
13. Sh. Jaswant Singh
14. Sh. Bal Kishan
15. Sh. Sardar Ali
16. Sh. Sukhdev Singh
17. Sh. M. Zaffar Abbas
18. L. Keshwanand.

Designation

Senior Supdt. of Police.

Supdt. of Police.

C.I.D. Supdt. New Delhi

Deputy Supdt. of Police, City.

Deputy Supdt. of Police. C.ID. Security.

Deputy Supdt. of Police. C.I.D. Prosecuting

Deputy Supdt. of Police.

Deputy Supdt. of Police. Office.

Prosecuting Inspector of Police.

C.I.D. Inspector of Police.

C.I.A. S.H.O. Hauz Qazi Inspector &

S.H.O. Kotwali. Distt.

Inspector of Police. City.

Inspector of Police. C.I.D.

Inspector & S.H.O. Faiz Bazar Police Station.

Inspector. Head Clerk. S.S.Ps Office.

Office date of posting to Delhi

Police Office Kashmere Gate. 1.5.44

C.I.D. Office. Kashmere Gate. 1.9.46

Police Office. Kashmere Gate. 11.5.45

Kotwali Police Station. Chandni Chowk. 28.7.45

C.I.D. Office Kashmere Gate 1.7.44

C.I.D. Office. Kashmere Gate 15.10.45

Police Office, Kashmere Gate 14.5.46.

Police Office Kashmere Gate. 1.7.31

Police Office Kashmere Gate. 3.3.46.

C.I.D. Office. Kashmere Gate. 25.4.44.

Kotwali Police Station. Chandni Chowk. 21.7.45.

Sadar Bazar Police Station 1.11.46.

Kotwali, Chandni Chowk. 27.9.45.

Kotwali Police Station. Chandni Chowk. 18.3.46.

C.I.D. Office. Kashmeri Gate. 5.4.46.

Faiz Bazar Police Station, 7.5.46.

Police Office, Kashmere Gate 22.11.46.

Residence

11, Alipore Road.

11, Alipore Road.

8, Rajpur Road,

Daryaganj.

8, Jantar Mantar Road, New Delhi.

54, Babar Lane, New Delhi.

Subzimandi,

Nawab Ganj,

Pul Bangash,

Subzimandi Police Lines,

Rajpur Road.

Nicholson Road, Chali Ganj, Kashmere Gate.

62, Ashoka Road, New Delhi.

Police Lines, Delhi.

Kotwali Police Station, Chandni Chowk,

Subzimandi.

19, Birla Flat, Qarol Bagh.

Faiz Bazar Police Station,

Babar Road, New Delhi.

Remarks

Under orders of transfer from Hisar to Delhi.

Notified Area

Name

19. Mr. S.G. Burton.
20. Mr. A.F.P. Hyde.
21. Mr. G.F. Corey.
22. S. Zamir-ul-Hassan.
23. Mr. A.H. Harrison.
24. M. Zulfiqar Ali.
25. S. Eqbal Hussain.

Designation

Traffic Inspector,

Inspector C.I.D. New Delhi.

Reserve Inspector.

District Inspector 'A'.

Inspector of Police.

Office and date of posting

Police Lines, Rajpur Road, 26.3.45.

Police Lines, Rajpur Road, 1.4.46.

Police Lines, Rajpur Road, 3.9.45.

Police Lines, Rajpur Road, 15.3.42.

Police Lines, Rajpur Road, 24.5.45.

Police Lines, Rajpur Road, 23.3.46.

Residence

19, Safdarjang Road, New Delhi.

25 Rajpur Road.

Rajpur Road,

Police Lines,

Rajpur Road,

Police Lines.

Rajpur Road,

Police Lines,

Rajpur Road.

Remarks

Under orders of transfer in G.O's office at the Personal Training Phillaur, returned to office. Acting from Mr. S.G.B. who is acting Training Camp Phillaur

507/46-H noted above D.S.P. of Police. Under orders of transfer from C.I.D. Punjab, Lahore to Delhi.

NEW DELHI

Name

26. Mr. Teani
27. S. Tek Singh
28. L. Ram Nath .
29. Sujan Singh
30. Agha Sultan Ahmad
31. Mr. I.J.B. Elder
32. Sh. Zeenat-Ullah
33. Mr Kraves
34. Ramparsahd.

Designation

Supdt. of Police, New Delhi,

Deputy Supdt. of Police, New Delhi.

Prosecuting Inspector of Police

I/c Viceroy's Police Guard,

Inspector of Police on Protection Duty,

Inspector of Police Delhi Cantonment,

Office and Date of Posting

Parliament Street Police Station 15.12.44

Parliament Street Police Station 1.9.45

Resident Magistrate's Court, New Delhi 2.4.44,

Parliament Street Police Station 17.9.45.

Parliament Street Police Station 24.4.46

H.E. the Viceroy's House 10.9.42.

Parliament Street Police Station, New Delhi 3.7.46.

Delhi Cantonment's Police Station 23.7.43.

Residence

22. Ashoka Road, New Delhi.

33. Gurdwara Road, New Delhi.

Sunder Bhawan,

CivilLines,

Parliament Street Police Station.

7. Babar Lane, New Delhi.

Viceregal Estate.

Parliament Street Police Station, New Delhi,

Birdwood Place, Delhi Cantonment.

APPENDIX II

A MEMORANDUM PRESENTED BY THE MUSLIM COMMUNITY TO THE GOVERNMENT OF INDIA

1. It is common knowledge that Sikhs, in considerable numbers, began to arrive in Delhi early this month. Many of them alighted from trains when they happened to stop for want of signal, as they often do, near the Bangash Bridge, situated in our locality. We noticed them both on account of their large numbers and their influx on what may be called a somewhat 'organized scale'. They were usually armed with swords and spears besides *kirpans* (daggers). According to all indications many of them took residence in our neighbouring mohallas.
2. We are not in a position to know whether the authorities deemed it proper or not to inquire into the reasons and objects of their influx on such a scale but they have remained a source of danger to us and a standing menace to our safety, especially in view of their parading of arms while moving about and passing through our mohallas. We brought all this to the notice of our elders and leaders.

* SOURCE: Home File No. 36/1947-C, Part B, 1947.

3. We were expecting that some suitable steps would be taken by the authorities against the swords and spears of the Sikhs on the occasion of "Anti Pakistan Day" on the 13th instant. But the authorities for reasons known only to them, took no such steps. We were greatly disappointed and feeling apprehensive, quite unarmed as we were. But fortunately the day passed off without any serious incident - according to our reading, simply because their top leaders wanted their demonstration to prove both successful and peaceful.
4. After that the "Pakistan Day" was coming on the 23rd March. Here again we were expecting that the authorities would move against the swords and spears of the Sikhs, if not against their *kirpans* (daggers). But disappointment was in store for us once again. The position on the morning of the 23rd was something like this: that the Sikhs were allowed to parade their swords (as distinct from their usual *kirpans*, daggers) in public thoroughfares, while the Musalmans were not allowed even lathis, nor were they allowed to go to the Urdu Park meeting in organized batches and in strength. The only source of reassurance for the Musalmans on that day was the pronouncements of the authorities about so-called elaborate arrangements for the protection of their lives and properties. But all this proved of no avail on the "Pakistan Day", when, according to the most reliable information available to us, some of armed Sikhs launched their offensive just in front of the Jama Masjid (on Pakistan Day meeting, which was presided by Mr. Liaqat Ali Khan, Finance Member in the Interim Government) wounding several Musalmans and killing them with

their swords, as also in Chandni Chowk in front of their Gurudwara, murdering, maiming Musalmans under the very nose of the City Police Headquarters. It was simply the extraordinary restraint exercised by the Musalmans under the influence of their leader and their appeals to maintain peace and help in the maintenance of order, even in the face of all provocations that saved Delhi from a major disaster that day.

5. Now, it was clearly the most urgent duty of the authorities to take suitable steps against aggressors and the people who had proved beyond any shadow of doubt to be the breakers of peace. Any just and impartial administration would and should have done that. But we do not know if anything has so far been done in this direction - the swords of the Sikhs are still outside the purview of the order under Section 144 Cr.P.C, while the Musalmans are not allowed even the *lathis* to protect and defend themselves.

6. What is happening in this ward, so far as the Musalmans are concerned, ever since the incidents of 23rd March, is most bewildering. They are being harassed and arrested without any apparent cause and their houses searched without bringing out anything incriminating. On the other side, in our neighbouring Hindu localities we do not notice activities of the authorities on such a scale.

7. To give just one instance of high handedness, we beg to submit that Muslim residents of these localities belong mostly to respectable and peaceful business communities of the wholesale market of Sadar Bazar and the Hide and Skin market. It is their long established practice that they go out in

the morning buying fruit and vegetables in the Mohalla Market for their household use. They were as usual busy in this after curfew hours on the morning of the 26th in the Kishan Gunj Mohalla when a party of police men arrived interfering, abusing and trying to disperse them. This was harassment pure and simple. When this was protested against by elder and respectable people they were abused and threatened with immediate arrest. As against this the Hindus and Sikhs, who armed with long swords stand guard there. But there is no one to check them.

Under the above circumstances, we are obliged to submit the following demands, which may kindly be granted immediately, without which we fear that tconfidence in the Local Administration will not be restored and peace and harmony will not be re-established.

(a) Musalmans, as also other communie ties, must be allowed to keep swords and spears just as the Sikhs are keeping them.

(b) People belonging to all communities (including Sikhs) must be treated and dealt with uniformly and without the least discrimination or favour, in the matter of parading in public all weapons, kirpans, swords or spears under Section 144 orders.

(c) Importance is being given to Muslim prayers and prayer in mosques during curfew hours.

(d) If the authorities are really following the policy of strict non-interference in matters of religion, and cannot interfere in the right of the Sikhs keeping kirpans with them, then a very reasonable course for the authorities will be: (i) to restrict the size of kirpans, (ii) to seal them so that the weapon cannot be drawn out without breaking the seal, as only the keeping of the kirpans (not its use, use against unarmed people) can be at any stretch of imagination be called a religious right, (iii) on the other side, the religious right of Musalmans to say their congregational prayers in mosques during curfew hours must be readily recognized.

(e) Persons, who were arrested when their houses were searched without finding anything incriminating, should be released forthwith and all proceedings against them withdrawn.

(f) Police must be directed to carry out searches only after giving due allowance for purdah observing ladies so that they could be able to observe *purdah*.

(g) Important key positions in the administration must be equally distributed between the Hindus and Musalmans, and Sikhs, whose preset representation bears no relation to the proportion of their population in Delhi, removed forthwith.

(h) An impartial enquiry by non-officials must be instituted immediately into the acts of omission and commission of the police ever since the Sikhs broke peace on 23rd March 1947.

We remain Sir Your Most Obedient Servants. Copies of the above forwarded to:

1. The Honourable Sardar V.B. Patel, Home Member, Government of India, New Delhi.

2. The Deputy Commissioner, Delhi.

3. The President, Delhi Provincial Muslim League, Urdu Bazar, Delhi.

APPENDIX III

The following persons did good work during September disturbances, in the Jamuna flood relief work in Delhi. The names of those who have done conspicuously good work are marked with a star.

September Riot

01.* L.Hanuman Parshad, Rais and Hony. Magistrate, Delhi.

02.* Dr. C.R. Jayna, Sub-Registrar and Hony. Magistrate, Delhi.

03.* Mir Mushtaq Ahmad.

04.* Mr. Aziz Hussain Buqqai.

05.* L. Padam Chand Jain.

06.* L. Des Raj Chaudhry.

07.* Mr. Jugal Kishore Khanna.

08.* L. Hem Chand Jain.

09.* Dr. Rattan Sharda.

10.* Mr. R.N. Aggarwal.

11.* Bava Bachitar Singh.

* SOURCE: File No. 129/147, D.C. Office.

12.* L. Desh Bandhu Gupta.
13.* Mr. B.D. Joshi.
14.* Mr. C.K. Nair.
15.* Mr. K.P. Shankar.
16. D. ShamNath.
17. Ch. SherJang.
18. J. JaswantRai.
19. Dr. Yudhvir Singh.
20. B. Ram Lal Verma.
21. Deputy Lal Jain.
22. Shree Shiv Charan Gupta.
23. Shree Raghbir Singh.
24. L. Ram Charan Aggarwal.
25. Shree Ganpat Ram Gupta.
26. Shree Ajit Dass Gupta.
27. Shree Ved Parkash Khanna.
28. Shree Jugal Ki shore Khanna.
29. Shree Radha Raman.
30. Shree Sanwal Dass.
31. Shree Narain Das Gupta.
32. Hari Kishan Gupta.
33. Shree Tara Chand Lohiya.
34. Shree Bishan Swaroop.
35. Shree Kanhiya Singh.
36. Mr. Hafizul Rehman.
37. Ch. MohdNaqqui.
38. Mr. Mohd. Ismail.
39. Mr. Lal Chand.
40. Shree Narsingham.
41. Shree Chandoo Lal.

42. Mr. Mohd. Faiz Ali.
43. L. Phul Chand Jain.
44. L. Ram Saran Chauhan.
45. Shree Gopi Nath Singh.
46. L. Bidhi Chand.
47. Ch.Raghu Nath Singh
48. Pt. Jai Dev Sharma.
49. Shree Richpal Singh Rana.
50. Mohdldris.
51. Mohd Ilyas.
52. Mr. Sheikh Allauddin.
53. Pr. Ram Partap.
54. Master Madho Ram.
55. Shree Durga Chand Kausik.
56. Shree Kalyan Singh.
57.
58.
59. L. Omkar Nath.
60. Shree Omkar Nath Sharma.
65. Shree R.D. Joshi.
68. Ch. Kanwal Singh.
69. Ch. Siri Ram.
70. Ch Hira Singh.
71. Shree Jagat Parkash.
72. Shree Chinta Mani.
73. Shree Vishwa Nath Shah, G.O.C., Congress Seva Dal.
74. Shree Roop Narain.
75. Shree Uma Shankar.
76. Shree Kati Kishore.

77. Shree Vijjay Singh.
78. Shree Lalte Parshad.
79. Shree Madan Mohan Yadav.
80. Shree Rattan Lal.
81. Shree Rameshar Nath Gupta.
82. Shree Jawala Parshad.
83. Shree Chhote Lal.
84. Shree Ranvir Singh.
85. Shree Pritam Singh.
86. Shree Vijjay Singh Bhardwaj.
87. Shree Sardar Singh.
88. Shree Richpal Singh.
89. Shree Sher Singh.
90. Shree Durga Parshad.
91. Shree Satya Narain Vaid.
92. Shree Sham Lal.
93. Shree Sham Lal Mehta.
94. Master Sham Lal.
95. Shree Mukh Nath.
96. Shree Bhagwan Dass alias Bhagwana.
97. Shree Suraj Parkash.
98. Shree Rash Bihari.
99. Shree Bansi Lal Sharma.
100. Shree Khairati Lal.
101. Shree Kishan Datt.
102. Shree Lakshmi Narain.
103. Shree Sukh Dev.
104. Shree Babu Ram Azad.
105. Shree Amar Singh.
106. Shree A.C. Nanda.

107. Shree Pokar Nath.
108. Shree Jugal Kishore.
109. Shree Ajit Singh Rye.
110. Shree Hargu Lal.
111. Shree Lakhpat Rai.
112. Shree Lila Devi.
113. Shree Sharda Singh.
114. Shree Ram Partap.
115. Shree Gulab Chand Jain.
116. Vaid Damodar Sarup.
117. ?

Special Magistrates

118. Mr. Deva Singh Randhawa.
119. Gyani Khem Singh.
120. Mr. Avinash Nayyar.
121. Mr. Mehraj Kishan.
122. Mr. S.K. Chaudhry.
123. Mr. Ranjit Singh.
124. Mr. G.B. Gupta.
125. R.B. Narain Dass.
126. Mr. R.S. Randhawa.
127. S. Partap Singh.
128. L Lakshmi Chand Jain.
129. Mr. Uttam Parkash Bansal.
130. Mr. P.N. Kukreja.
131. Mr. Sadhev.
132. Mr. Halim Jung.
133. Mr. B.L. Malhotra.
134. Mr. Ranjit Singh Narula.
135. Mr. Hem Chander Jain.
136. Mr. Hem Chandra Rai.

137. Pt. Shiv Lai Sharma.
138. Ch. Ghazi Ram.
139. Mr. E. Abbasi.
140. Mr. Hilal Ahmad Zuberi.
141. Professor Ramdhan.
142. Mr. Puran Singh Mandla.
143. Mr. Brahma Parkash.
144. Mr. Sher Jung.
145. Mr. A.S. Bhaatnagar.
146. Ch. Hukam Singh.
147. Dr. R. Chandra.
148. Mr. Om Parkash.
149. Mr. Sikandar Bakht.
150. Mr. Om Parkash.
151. Mr. M.N. Masud.
152. Mr. Habib Ullah.
153. Mr. Kamal Ud Din.
154. Mr. Munish Chander.
155. Mr. Ram Parshad.
156. Mr. J.N. Sahni.
157. L. Roop Narain Khanna.
158. L. Ram Charan Aggarwal.
159. L. Jagan Nath Singh.
160. L. Brij Bhushan Saran.
161. Mr. Daljit Singh.
162. Mr. Ram Nath Kalia Shanker.
163. Mr. Neuttan Nand Kishor.

Flood Relief

1. Mr. Neuttan Nand Kishor.
2. Dr. P.R. Bami.
3. Ch. Hira Singh.
4. Mr. Jagat Parkash.

5. Mr. Shiv Charan Gupta.
6. Mr. Chintta Munni.
7. Mr. Yageshwar Datta.
8. Mr. Jagdish Mitar Chopra.
9. Mr. Ram Nath Jain.

Refugee Relief

1. Shrimati Memo Bai.
2. Mr. Natwar Lai.
3. Mrs. Ramesh Mehta.
4. Ch. Ajit Singh.
5. Mr. Raj Kishan.
6. Mr. R.D. Jain.
7. Mrs. Savitri Dulari Lal.
8. Mr. Mangat Ram.
9. Mr. Girdhari Lal.
10. Mr. G.R.S. Yadhba.
11. Mr. Yash Pal.
12. Mr. Charanji Lal.
13. Mr. Dharam Dev.
14. Mr. L.K. Sarkar.
15. Mr. Roshan Lal.
16. Mr. Udhe Vir.
17. Mr. Tula Ram.
18. Mrs. Vidya Datta.
19. Shree Savita Behan.
20. Mr. Nahrain Lal.

APPENDIX IV

Here is a list of the Special Magistrates who were appointed .during the recent emergency. It is not possible to comment at any length on the work done by each of these magistrates but the names of those who according to the information and knowledge did exceptionally good work and thus possess sufficient qualifications for being appointed as Hony. Magistrates:

1. **Mir Mushtaq Ahmed:** He is a man of sterling worth and proven integrity. He is one of the few Muslims who rose above communalism at all times. He has been very energetic as Special Magistrate and was prepared to risk his own life by going to the worst affected localities.
2. **Bava Bachittar Singh:** He is a selfless worker, who always takes active interest in social welfare work of all kinds. He was particularly helpful in organizing the clean-up campaign in Paharganj area after the recent disturbances.
3. **Mr. Hem Chander Jain:** He commands considerable respect and influence among the Hindus in Sadar Bazar area and is a Municipal Commissioner. He has been working as an Arbitrator in the cloth dealers' disputes with considerable success for a fairly long time. He

is a public-spirited individual, who should be encouraged. He has received some college education and is a fluent Urdu speaker.

4. **Ranjit Narula:** He is one of the leading civil lawyers of Delhi and has also considerable knowledge and experience of criminal courts. I understand that he is appointed as Hony. Magistrate.
5. **Mr. C.B.Gupta:** I understand that he has already been recommended for appointment as Hon. Magistrate. He is a responsible person and, is very keen to be helpful to the administration and to use his influence on the right side.
6. **Lieut. Puran Singh Mondle:** He has been very zealous with being indiscreet in the discharge of his duties as a Special Magistrate. He was prepared to be posted at any police station day or night. This cannot be said of all Special Magistrates.
7. **Mr. Daljit Singh:** He is the intelligent young man, who belongs to a most eminent Sikh family of Delhi being a son of S. Sobha Singh of I-A Queensway, New Delhi. He was very energetic in patrolling and other duties entrusted to him as a Special Magistrate. He is highly educated and is anxious to be useful to the administration.
8. **Seth Gauri Shanker Goenka:** He was appointed as Special Magistrate at a fairly late stage during the last disturbances. He, however, proved his worth during the Ram Lila and Id celebrations when he was on duty with the City Magistrate, Kr. Mohinder Singh Bedi, whose certificate regarding him is attached.

APPENDIX V

BARTAMAN HINDU-MUSSALMAN SAMSYA

Sarat Chandra Chattopadhyay

[First presented as a speech at the Bengal Provincial Conference of 1926, the text of this essay later appeared in Hindu Sangha, 19 Ashwin 1333. A translation is given below]*

The Current Hindu-Muslim Problem

A notion need not be correct simply because large numbers of people assert it with great conviction. No matter what the strength of their numbers and despite the clamour of their combined voice, what the crowds proclaim is not necessarily true. The unceasing cacophony of voices shouting in unison forces people into believing what they hear. But this is propaganda. In the last great war, both sides accepted as true the falsehood that killing each other is man's duty merely because much ink has flowed and many voices have been raised to persuade them of this untruth. The few

*Translation taken from the book, *Bengal Divided,* by Joya Chatterji, Cambridge University Press, 1995.

who challenged this view and attempted to speak the truth were subjected to endless ridicule and humiliation. But times have changed. Having undergone much pain and sorrow, people today have realized there was little truth in much that was said at that time.

So it was some years ago in this country, at the time when Mahatma Gandhi launched his non-violent Non-Cooperation movement. Many leaders loudly proclaimed that Hindu-Muslim unity had to be achieved, whatever the cost. They wanted it not only because it was good in itself, but because we without it, to dream of Swaraj and Independence was mere foolishness. If they had been asked why it was 'foolishness', who knows what they would have answered. But in speeches, through writing and shouting, it achieved the status of a self-evident truth. And nobody except a fool would dare to question it.

Then Hindus lost everything in an attempt to find the magic grail of togetherness. Countless time and energy was wasted in this pursuit. It resulted in the Mahatma's Khilafat Movement and in Deshbandhu's Pact, whose hollowness is unsurpassed in Indian politics. There was at least a semblance of an excuse for the Pact because *willy-nilly* it was a compromise suited to the times which aimed to defeat the Bengal Government in Council. But the Khilafat movemet, from the Hindu side, was not only pointless, it was false. Battles fought for a false cause can never be won. And the lie of Khilafat, like an unbearably heavy stone tied around the neck, dragged the Non-Cooperation movement to its destruction.

We want Swaraj. We want freedom from the yoke of foreign rule. The British may put up a case against this demand of the Indian people, but their case will not stand in the court of world opinion. Whether or not we succeed, the struggle for our birthright is noble, and those who lose their lives in this struggle will go to heave. There is no one on earth who will not accept this truth.

But 'we want Khilafat'. What sort of talk was this? A country with which India had no connection - we did not even know what its people ate, wore or looked like - a country that was ruled by Turkey in the past! And once Turkey was defeated in the war and the Sultan was sent back, the colonized Indian Muslim community childishly insisted on his return. Was this reasonable?

In reality, this was also a pact. Or rather it was a bribe. 'We want Swaraj and you want Khilafat - so come, let us unite. We will offer our heads to be broken for Khilafat, and you will raise the slogan of Swaraj'. But to the one demand for Swaraj the British Government paid no heed, and in reply to the other the Caliph for whom the Khilafat movement had been launched was expelled from Turkey. Thus, the Khilafat movement proved entirely meaningless and insubstantial, in its hollowness it not only destroyed itself, but it also killed India's independence movement. Can one ever bribe, entice or delude people into joining a freedom struggle? And indeed if you can will you ever win victory? I do not think this can ever be possible.

The one who laboured hardest for this [Hindu-Muslim unity] was Mahatmaji himself. No one else had as much hope, and no one else felt so cheated. In those days, Muslim politicians were at his right hand

and at his left, they were his eyes and his ears. My goodness, was there ever such a spectacle? His last attempt for Hindu-Muslim unity was his twenty-one day fast at Delhi. He is a simple god-fearing man: perhaps he thought that by showing a readiness to suffer, they would take pity on him [and relent]. Somehow his life was saved. His dearly beloved friend Mr Mohammed Ali was the one who was most disturbed, it all happened before his eyes. Shedding crocodile tears, he said, 'Oh what a good man is this Mahatmaji! I want to do something really helpful for him. So let us first go to Mecca, then make an oblation to the Pir, then read the Kalma, and make him renounce the infidel religion'. On hearing this, the disillusioned Mahatma cried, 'Let the earth swallow me'.

The truth is that if Muslims ever say that they want to unite with Hindus, there is no greater hoax. The Muslims came to India to plunder it, not to establish a kingdom.

They were not satisfied merely with looting, they destroyed temples, they demolished idols, they raped women. The insult to other religions and the injury to humanity were unimaginable.

Even when they became kings they could not liberate themselves from these loathsome desires. Even Akbar, who was famed for his tolerance, was no better than notorious emperors like Aurangzeb. But today it seems that their practices have become an addiction. Many argue that the monstrous events at Pabna were the work of mullahs from the West, who excited the innocent and uneducated Muslim peasants and instigated these awful deeds. But if, in the same way, a party of Hindu priests were to arrive in a Hindumajorty area and try to incite the docile Hindu peasantry to burn the homesteads, loot the property and insult the women of their innocent Muslim neighbours, then the same unlettered Hindu peasantry would immediately declare them mad and drive them away from the village.

Why does this happen? Is it simply the result of illiteracy? If learning is simply knowing how to read and write, there is little difference between Hindu and Muslim peasants and labourers. But if the essence of learning is breadth of mind and culture at one's very heart, then there is no comparison between the two communities. When journalists raise the question of the abduction of Hindu women, why are the Muslim leaders silent? When people of their community regularly commit such grave crimes why do they not protest? What is the meaning of their silence? To my mind the meaning is crystal clear. It is only a sense of decorum that prevents them from admitting openly that far from protesting given the opportunity, they would commit the same crimes themselves.

Unity can only be realized among equals. Many of us hope to establish a parity of learning [between Hindus and Muslims] but I do not. A thousand years has not been enough time to achieve this, nor will another millennium suffice. If to expel the British, this is our only resource, then Independence will have to wait. There is much else to do. Some hoped that with Khilafat and with the Das Pact, they might be able to sweet-talk Muslims into the freedom struggle, but the majority did not. There are those who argue that there is no teacher like grief and despair, that when Muslims suffered continuous humiliation at the hands of the imperialist, they would be awakened and would fight shoulder to shoulder with Hindus for Swaraj. But they are mistaken, because they have not taken into account the fact that the very ability to sense humiliation is itself a product of learning. While a man like Deshbandhu burned with humiliation I [a lesser mortal] was uaffected. More importantly, those who feel no horror while expressing the weak can feel no shame when they grovel before the mighty. So why are we deceiving ourselves? 'Hindu-Muslim unity' is a bombastic phrase. At different times, many such phrases have been bandied about but they serve no purpose. We must sacrifice this illusion. It is useless for us to try to shame Bengali Muslims by saying that seven generations ago they were Hindus, therefore they are related to us by blood: fratricide is a sin, so show little pity. To my mind there is nothing more dishonourable than begging for pity and groveling for unity. In this country and abroad, I have several Christian friends. Either they or their forefathers adopted a new faith. But unless they tell you themselves that they are Christians it is impossible to tell them apart from us, or to think that they are not still our brothers and sisters. I knew a Christian lady once. She died young, but even so, there are few who have earned as much respect in their lifetimes.

But Muslims? I had a Brahmin cook once. He sacrificed his religion in order to indulge his passion for a Muslim woman. One year later, he had changed his name, his dress and even his nature. The very face that God gave him had changed beyond recognition. And this is not an isolated instance. Those who know something about village life knows that this sort of thing happens frequently. And in the matter of aggression, these new converts put their Muslim co-religionists to shame.

The problem before Hindus, therefore, is not to bring about this unnatural union between Hindus and Muslims. Their task is to achieve unity within their own community, and to bring an end to the folly of those practicing Hindus (Hindu dharmaablambi) who insult some people by called them 'low caste'. Even more pressing is the need for Hindus to think about how they may let the [religious] truth within them blossom like a flower in their everyday lives and public behaviour. Those who think do not speak those who speak do not act and those who act are not accepted. If this evil is not checked, even God will not be able to mend the countless holes that are being punched into the fabric of the community.

This is the problem and this is the duty. There is no point in wailing or beating our breasts because Hindu-Muslim unity has not come about. If we stop our own crying, we may be able to hear crying from their quarters.

Hindustan is the homeland of the Hindus. Therefore it is the duty of the Hindus alone to free this nation from the chains of servitude. Muslims look towards Turkey and Arabia, their hearts are not in India. What is the use of bemoaning this fact? To appeal to them in the name of the Soil of Mother India is as pointless as talking to a brick wall. Today it is vital that we understand this point that this work is the work only of Hindus, and no one else. There is no need to get agitated counting how numerous is the Muslim population. Numbers are not the ultimate truth in this world. There are greater truths, in whose scale of values the arithmetic of counting heads has no place.

All that I have said about Hindu-Muslim unity may

be a bitter pill to swallow. But this is no cause for alarm. Nor is there any reason to call me a traitor. I am not suggesting that I will not be pleased if ties of mutual respect and affection were to grow up between these two neighbouring communities. All I am saying is that if this does not come about, and if there are no signs that it is likely to ever come about, it is useless to weep. Nor is it helpful to believe that such a failure would mean the end of the world. It has been repeated so often that we have come to believe that it is the only truth, and that there is no other way. But are we actually achieving anything? No. All that we do is compile lists of all instances of the cruelty and hostility of Muslims towards us, all that we say is this: 'You have killed us you have broken our idols, destroyed our temples and kidnapped our women. In this you have been very unjust, and have caused us great pain. We cannot continue to live like this'.

Do we ever say more than this, or do more than this? We have accepted without hesitation that it is our role to bring about 'togetherness' and their responsibility to stop oppressing us. But in truth, the roles should be reversed. It is our job to put a stop to their cruelty, and, if anything remains of 'Hindu-Muslim unity', it is their duty to bring it about.

But how can our country be freed? I ask you this - can our countr be freed by fraud? When Hindus come forward and vo.w to free their country, then it will matter little whether a few dozen Muslims lend their support or not. The Muslims will never truly believe that India's freedom will bring them freedom too. They will only accept this truth when their obsession with their religion weakens. Then they will understand that whatever one's religion, to be proud of fanaticism is a matter of shame, there is no greater barbarism than this. But there is a long way to go before they will understand this. Unless all the people all over the world unite to educate the Muslims, it is doubtful that their eyes will ever be opened. Moreover, do all the people of a nation ever come forward together to fight for its freedom? Is it ever possible or even necessary? When America fought for her independence, the majority of her people supported the British. How many Irish people supported the Irish freedom movement? The Bolshevik government that is in power in Russia has not the support of even one per cent of the people. Human beings are not animals; crowds alone do not establish what is true. Intense spiritual endeavour alone can identify and establish the truth.

The burden of this single-minded devotion lies on the shoulders of the male youths of our nation. It is not their job to scheme for Hindu-Muslim unity. Nor is it their duty to waste their time applauding those political leaders who are howling hopelessly for this unity. There are many things in this world that can be attained only by sacrificing them first. Hindu-Muslim unity is one among these. I feel that if we sacrifice this hope and get down to work, we will see proof of this. In that event, unity will not be the outcome of the efforts of one side, but will be the result of a shared desire sincerely felt by both sides.[1]

1 Source: Haripada Ghosh (ed.), *Sarat Rachana Samagra* ("Collected Works of Sarat Chandra Chattopadhyay'), III, Calcutta, 1989.

SELECT BIBLIOGRAPHY

PRIMARY SOURCES

Fiction Relating to Partition

Ali, Ahmed, *Twilight in Delhi* (1940, Delhi, 1991).

Bhalla, Alok, *Stories on the Partition of India* (Delhi, 1994) 3 volumes.

Francisco Jason, 'In the Hat of the Fratricide: the Literature of India's Partition Burning Freshly', review article in *Annual of Urdu Studies* (1997).

Hasan, Khalid tr. *Kingdom's End and Other Stories* (London, 1987).

Manto ke numaindah afsane, comp. Atahar Parvez (Aligarh 1981).

Memon, Muhammad Umad, ed. *An Epic Unwritten. The Penguin Book of Partition Stories;* (Delhi, 1998).

Masoom Raza, Rahi, *Aadha gaon* (Delhi, 1966).

Masoom Raza, Rahi, *Feuding Families of Village Gangauli,* tr. Gillian Wright (Delhi, 1995).

Sahni, Bhishma, *'Amritsar aa gaya'* in *Kitne Toba Tek Singh. Bharat vibhajan ki das Kahaniyan* (Delhi, 1987).

Contemporary Writings Documents, Speeches and Memoirs

Abbasi, Jalil, *Kya din the* (Delhi, 1987).

Ambedkar, B.R., *Pakistan, or the Partition of India* (Bombay, 1946).

Azad, Abul Kalam, *India Wins Freedom: The Complete Version* (Madras, 1988).

Aziz, K.K., *The Historical Background of Pakistan, 1857-1947: an Annotated Digest of Source Material* (Karachi, 1970).

Barelvi, Ebadad, *Azadi ke saaye mein* (Lahore, 1988).

Bose, Sarat Chandra, *I Warned My Countrymen. Being the Collected Works 1945-50 of Sarat Chandra Bose* (Calcutta, 1968).

Chaudhuri, Nirad C., *Thy Hand, Great Anarch! India 1921-1952* (London, 1987).

Das, Durga, ed., *Sardar Patel's Correspondence, 1945-50*, vols, iv-v (Ahmedabad, 1972-3).

Dehlavi, Shahi Ahmad, *Dilli ki bipta* (Naya Daur, 1948), reprinted in Mumtaz Shirin, ed., *Zulmat-i-nimroz* (Karachi, 1990).

Gandhi, M.K., *Collected Works of Mahatma Gandhi*, various volumes (Delhi).

Hameed, Syeda Saiyidai, *India's Maulana. Selected Speeches and Writings of Maulana Abul Kalam Azad* (Delhi, 1990).

Hasan, Mushirul Hasan, ed., *India Partitioned. The Other Face of Freedom* (Delhi, 1995).

Khosla G.D., *Memory's Gay Chariot. An Autobiographical Narrative* (Delhi, 1985).

Stern Reckoning. A Survey of the Events Leading up to and Following the Partition of India (1949; reprinted Delhi, 1989).

Moon, Penderel, *Divide and Quit. An Eyewitness Account of the Partition of India* (Delhi, 1998).

Nehru, Jawaharlal, *Glimpses of World History*, vol. II (1934; 2nd edn, Bombay, 1961).

Selected Works of Jawaharlal Nehru, 2nd series, vol. I (Delhi, 1984).

Pyarelal, *Mahatma Gandhi. The Last Phase,* vol. II (Ahmedabad, 1958).

Qidwai, Begum Anees, *Azadi ki chhaon mein,* Hindi tr., Nur Nabi Abbasi (Delhi, 1990).

Sherwani, Latif Ahmed, ed., *Pakistan Resolution to Pakistan, 1940-1947. A Selection of Documents Presenting the Case for Pakistan* (Karachi, 1969; reprinted Delhi, 1985).

Singh, Kirpal, comp., *Shaheedian* (Amritsar, 1964?).

Stree Shakti Sanghataa, 'We Were Making History ... 'Life Stories of Women in the Telengana People's Struggle (Delhi, 1989).

Talib, Gurbachan Singh, comp., *Muslim League Attack on Sikhs and Hindus in the Punjab, 1947* (Amritsar, 1950; reprinted, Delhi, 1991).

Tandon, Prakash, *Punjabi Century, 1857-1947* (Berkeley and Los Angeles, 1968).

Tuker, Francis, *While Memory Serves* (London, 1950).

Zaidi, A.M., ed., *Congress Presidential Addresses*. Volume 5; 1940-85 (Delhi, 1989). ed., *The Story of the Congress Pilgrimage,* Volume 4: 1940-55 (Delhi, 1990).

Zaidi, Z.H., ed., *Quaid-i-Azam Mohammad Ali Jinnah Papers. Prelude to Pakistan.* 20 Fbruary - 2 June 1947, 1st series, vol. I, part I (Islamabad, 1993).

Private Papers

Shyama Prasad Mookerjee Papers (Nehru Memorial Museum and Library) (NMML)

All India Congress Committee Papers (NMML).

Akhil Bharatiya Hindu Mahasabha Papers (NMML).

D.C. Office File, Delhi Province.Home Political Proceedings (National Archives of India) (NAI).

Census of India 1931 and 1941.

Newspapers

1. *The Hindustan Times*, New Delhi.
2. *The Dawn*, Faiz Bazaar Road, Delhi.
3. *The National Call*, Mori Gate, Delhi.
4. *The Janata Weekly*, Connaught Place, New Delhi.
5. *The Daily Tej*, Naya Bazaar, Delhi.
6. *The Riyasat*, Charkhewalan, Chawri Bazaar, Delhi.
7. *The Ansari*.
11. *The Swarajya*.

SECONDARY SOURCES

Ahmed, Rafiuddin, *The Bengal Muslims 1871-1906. A Quest for Identity*, New Delhi, 1981.

Ambedkar, B.R., *Gandhi and Gandhism*, Jullunder, 1970.

Anderson, Benedict, *Imagined Communities. Reflections on the Origins and Spread of Nationalism*, London, 1990.

Bagchi, Amiya Kumar, *Private Investment in India 1900-1939*, Madras, 1972.

Bak, J.M. and Benecker, G. (eds.), *Religion and Rural Revolt*, Manchester, 1984.

Bhattacharya, J.N., *Hindu Castes and Sects*, Calcutta, 1973. Bose,

Sarat Chandra, *I Warned My Countrymen. Being the Collected Works 1945-50 of Sarat Chandra Bose*, Calcutta, 1968.

Breuilly, John, *Nationalism and the State*, Manchester, 1985.

Broomfield, J.H., *Elite Conflict in a Plural Society. Twentieth-Century Bengal*, Berkeley, 1968.

Chakrabarty, Bidyut, *Subhas Chandra Bose and Middle-Class Radicalism. A Study in Indian Nationalism*, London, 1990.

Chandra, Bipan, *The Rise and Growth of Economic Nationalism in India*, New Delhi, 1966.

Chandra, Bipan, *Communalism in Modern India*, New Delhi, 1984.

Chatterjee, Bhola, *Aspects of Bengal Politics in the 1930s,* Calcutta, 1969.

Chatterjee, Partha, *Nationalist Thought and the Colonial World: A Derivative Discourse,* New Delhi, 1986.

Chatterjee, Partha and Pandey, Gyanendra (eds.), *Subaltern Studies,* Delhi, 1992.

Chaudhuri, Nirad, C. *Thy Hand Great Anarch! India, 1921-1952,* London, 1987. *The Autobiography of an Unknown Indian,* London, 1988.

Cohen, Anthony P., *The Symbolic Construction of Community,* London, 1985.

Cohn, B.S. and Singer, M., *Structure and Change in Indian Society,* Chicago, 1968.

Collins, Larry and Lapierre, Dominique, *Freedom at Midnight,* London, 1975.

Das, Suranjan, *Communal Riots in Bengal, 1905-1947,* New Delhi, 1991.

Dixit, Prabha, *Communalism: A Struggle for Power,* New Delhi, 1974.

Hwing, Katherine P., *Shari 'at and Ambiguity in South Asian Islam,* New Delhi, 1988.

Freitag, Sandria B., *Collective Action and Community. Public Arenas and the Emergence of Communalism in North India,* Berkeley, Los Angeles and Oxford, 1989.

Gandhi, Rajmohan, *Understanding the Muslim Mind,* New Delhi, 1988.

Geertz, Clifford, *The Interpretation of Cultures,* New York, 1973.

Giddens, Anthony, *The Class Structure of Advanced Societies,* London, 1973.

Gilmartin, David, *Empire and Islam. Punjab and the Making of Pakistan,* Berkeley, 1988.

Gopal, Sarvepalli (ed.), *The Anatomy of a Confrontation. The Babri Masjid-Ramjanmabhumi Issue,* New Delhi, 1991.

Hasan, Mushirul (ed.), *Communal and Pan-Islamic Trends in Colonial India,* New Delhi, 1985.

Hobsbawm, Eric ad Ranger, Terence (eds.), *The Invention of Tradition,* Cambridge, 1984.

Holyoake, G.J., *The Origin and Nature of Secularism,* London, 1896.

Hunt, Alan (ed.), *Class and Class Structure,* London, 1977.

Hunter, W.W., *The Indian Mussalmans,* London, 1876.

Inden, Ronald, *Imagining India,* Cambridge, Mass., 1990.

Ioescu, Gita and Gellner Ernest (eds.), *Populism. Its Meaning and National Characteristics,* London, 1969.

Jalal, Ayesha, *The Sole Spokesman. Jinnah, the Muslim League and the Demand for Pakistan,* Cambridge, 1985.

Kabir, Humayun, *Muslim Politics 1906-47 and Other Essays,* Calcutta, 1969.

Khaliquzzaman, Choudhury, *Pathway to Pakistan,* Lahore, 1961.

Kopf, David (ed.), *Bengal Regional Identity,* East Lansing, Mich., 1969.

Kumar, Ravinder, *Essays in the Social History of Modern India,* Calcutta, 1986.

Kumar, Ravinder, *Language and Symbolic Power* (translated by Gino Raymond and Matthew Adamson), Cambridge, 1992.

Leach, Edmund and Mukherjee, S.N. (eds.), *Elites in South Asia,* Cambridge, 1970.

Low, D.A. (ed.), *The Indian National Congress. Centenary Hindsights,* New Delhi, 1988. Macpherson, Kenneth, *The Muslim Microcosm. Calcutta, 1918-1985,* Wiesbaden, 1974.

McGuire John, *The Making of a Colonial Mind. A Quantitative Study of the Bhadralok in Calcutta, 1857-1885,* Canberra, 1983.

McLane, John R., *Indian Nationalism and the Early Congress,* Princeton, 1977.

Moore, R.J., *Churchill Cripps and India, 1939-1945*, Oxford, 1978.

Moore, R.J., *Escape from Empire. The Attlee Government and the Indian Problem*, Oxford, 1982.

Moore, R.J., *Endgames of Empire. Studies of Britain's Indian Problem*, New Delhi, 1988.

Mountbatten, Louis, *Reflections on the Transfer of Power and J. Nehru*, Cambridge, 1968.

Mujeeb, N., *The Indian Muslims*, London, 1969.

Nanda, B.R., (ed.), *Essays in Modern Indian History*, New Delhi, 1980.

Nehru, Jawaharlal, *The Discovery of India*, New Delhi, 1986.

Page, David, *Prelude to Partition. The Indian Muslims and the Imperial System of Control 1920-1932*, Delhi, 1982.

Pandey, Gyanendra, *The Ascendancy of the Congress in Uttar Pradesh 1926-34 A Study in Imperfect Mohiulization*, New Delhi, 1978.

Pandey, Gyanendra, *The Construction of Communalism in Colonial North India*, New Delhi, 1990.

Panigrahi, D.N. (ed.), *Economy, Society and Politics in India*, New Delhi, 1985.

Robb, Peter and Taylor, David (eds.), *Rule, Protest, Identity. Aspects of Modern South Asia*, London, 1978.

Robinson, F.C.R., *Separatism among Indian Muslims. The Politics of the United Provinces' Muslims, 1860-1923*, Cambridge, 1974.

Sarkar, Sumit, *The Swadeshi Movement in Bengal, 1903-1908*, New Delhi, 1973.

Sarkar, Sumit, *Modern India 1885-1947*, New Delhi, 1983.

Sarkar, Sumit, 'Popular' Movements and 'Middle Class' Leadership in Late Colonial India: Perspectives and Problems of a 'History From Below, Calcutta, 1985.

Sarkar, Sumit, *A Critique of Colonial India*, Calcutta, 1985.

Shaikh, Farzana, *Community and Consensus in Islam: Muslim*